SEPARATING
PARENTS
AND
ADOLESCENTS

SEPARATING PARENTS AND ADOLESCENTS

INDIVIDUATION IN THE FAMILY

HELM STIERLIN M.D., PH.D.

Jason Aronson / New York and London

The quotations from *Life* magazine, March 17, 1972, on pp. 29–30 are reprinted by permission of Time, Inc. Copyright © 1972, Time, Inc.

Grateful acknowledgment is due these publications for their permission to reprint material by the author that appeared in their pages: *Archives of General Psychiatry*, the *British Journal of Medical Psychology*, the *International Journal of Psycho-Analysis*, and *Excerpta Medica*.

ISBN 0-87668-477-0

Stierlin, Helm.
   Separating parents and adolescents.

   Bibliography: p.
   Includes indexes.
   1. Problem families—United States. 2. Parents and
   child—United States. 3. Runaway youth—United States.
I. Title.
HV699.S74 1981   362.8'2   81-12860   AACR2

Manufactured in the United States of America.

FOR MY MOTHER

Contents

Foreword to the New Edition

Since the first publication of *Separating Parents and Adolescents* in 1974 the interactional concepts described in that book have further evolved. At the same time, my notions about the therapy best suited to the troubled adolescent and his or her family have changed. It therefore made sense to enlarge this new edition by adding a chapter outlining the new theoretical developments and their implications for the therapy of adolescents and their families. Readers who want to familiarize themselves further with these topics might do so by turning to *Psychoanalysis and Family Therapy* (New York: Jason Aronson, 1977) and *The First Interview with the Family* by Helm Stierlin, Ingeborg Rücker-Embden, Norbert Wetzel, and Michael Wirsching (New York: Brunner/ Mazel, 1980).

Helm Stierlin, M.D., Ph.D.

Introduction

When the prodigal son returned home, he told his father, according to Luke 15: 21–32:

. . . "Father I have sinned against heaven and before you; I am no longer worthy to be called your son." But the father said to his servants, "Bring quickly the best robe, and put it on him; and put a ring on his hand, and shoes on his feet; and bring the fatted calf and kill it, and let us eat and make merry; *for this my son was dead, and is alive again; he was lost, and is found.*" [Luke 15: 21–24; author's italics]

Whereupon the elder son became angry and complained to his father, "Lo, these many years I have served you, and I never disobeyed your command; yet you never gave me a kid, that I might make merry with my friends. But when this son of yours came, who has devoured your living with harlots, you killed for him the fatted calf!" And he said to him, "Son, you are always with me, and all that is mine is yours. It was fitting to make merry and be glad, for this your brother was dead, and is alive; he was lost and is alive; he was lost and is found." [Luke 15; 29–32]

This story stakes out the main theme of this book: the drama of separating parents and children; a drama played for the highest stakes. Death and rebirth, losing and refinding what one holds dearest, deepest distress and joy, and conflict and reconciliation, are its elements.

These elements hide questions concerning the nature of

love, of obedience, and of mutual growth and liberation in families. For example, we might ask: Was the son who disobeyed his father more loved only because he was deemed dead and returned unexpectedly, *or was he loved more because he, in his very disobedience, was more deeply obedient than his well-behaved brother?* Could he perhaps have sensed that his father's life was shallow and lacking in excitement and that he, in becoming profligate, could vicariously provide such missing excitement? Could he have sensed that he, by leaving and returning home and by causing his father agony and pain, could trigger his father's long overdue growth and individuation? In brief, could he, *by overtly defying his father, covertly have fulfilled his father's deepest expectations —hidden, disowned, and ambiguous though these might have been?* It is questions such as these that I shall take up in this book.

Today, the prodigal son would be called a runaway, and his story has become newly relevant. For there are now approximately between six hundred thousand and a million American teenage children who run away from their homes every year. As with the prodigal son, their actions are cast into relief by the behavior of their nonrunaway siblings and, most importantly, by that of their parents. These runaways, their siblings, and their parents allow us therefore to study the separation process as if under a magnifying glass. Hence, I shall, again and again, deal with the runaway phenomenon.

This book draws on many years of psychotherapeutic and psychoanalytic contacts with separating parents and adolescents and also draws on a study at the National Institute of Mental Health begun almost six years ago.* The study focused originally on "underachievers" of both sexes and included

---

* Those findings of the study that enter into this book have already appeared in various scientific journals.

forty families. I assumed that so-called underachievers had a greater-than-normal chance to end up mentally disturbed and I intended to study the forces that either prevented or fostered such an outcome. My colleagues and I admitted to the program seriously underachieving adolescents whose ages ranged from fourteen to sixteen. All families participated in conjoint family therapy of no less than three months' duration. Over the ensuing five years, follow-up interviews were carried out. As the project developed, it changed from an outpatient to an inpatient program. The troubled adolescents received individual therapy while the whole family was seen at least once a week in family therapy. Also, we offered couple therapy to parents, individual therapy to siblings (if advisable and possible), and an intense milieu program to the hospitalized adolescent(s). Additionally, all participating family members took part in diagnostic interviews and various other research procedures.

After the program had been underway for about two years, the subtle dynamics of the separation process began to puzzle and preoccupy me increasingly. At about the same time, I became intrigued by the growing number of runaways who passed through the program. It was these runaways—as well as their nonrunaway siblings—and, above all, their parents, who then illuminated for me probably the most crucial aspects of adolescent separation.

Gradually, a framework emerged which made possible a deeper and more complex understanding of adolescent separation than seemed feasible within existing theories. This framework opened up new therapeutic perspectives—for disturbed adolescent runaways, for nonrunaways, and for their parents—and it allowed me to see in a new light such major mental disturbances as schizophrenia, sociopathy, and narcissism.

In the following chapters I shall develop this conceptual framework and shall illustrate it with clinical examples. As a sort of sketch map, for the unprepared reader, I want at this point to outline its central features.

On all levels, the separation process is shaped by the interaction of centripetal and centrifugal forces which reveal a relational dialectic. A first level concerns the life situation and marriage of middle-aged parents. Where centripetal forces dominate, parents become glued to each other in suffocating closeness; where centrifugal forces prevail, the spouses can breathe more freely, but often become interpersonally dislodged and uprooted. The interplay of centripetal and centrifugal forces in marriage also shapes the separation between the generations. This intergenerational separation—of which intergenerational conflict is only one aspect—is the core theme of this book. In order to develop it, I employ the concept of *transactional modes*. Throughout all phases of separation, these modes reflect the interplay and/or relative dominance of the above centripetal and centrifugal forces. As covert organizing structures, they shape the more obvious and specific child-parent interactions. When age-appropriate transactional modes are out of phase, too intense, or inappropriately mixed with other modes, mutual individuation and separation between parent and child will suffer.

I distinguish the three major modes of *binding, delegating,* and *expelling.*

Where the *binding mode* prevails, the parents interact with their offspring in ways that keep the latter tied to the parental orbit and locked in the "family ghetto."

Where the *delegating mode* is dominant, the child may move out of the parental orbit but remains tied to his parents by the long leash of loyalty. This delegate must then fulfill missions for his parents (e.g., the mission to provide vicarious excitement) that embroil him in various forms of conflict.

Where, finally, the *expelling mode* prevails, parents enduringly neglect and reject their children and consider them nuisances and hindrances to their own goals. A strong centrifugal force pushes many of these children into premature separations.

All these modes, I shall show, reflect and trigger different forms of running and not running away. Equipped with this conceptual model, I turn in Part II to problems of schizophrenia and waywardness. I consider these to be extremes of the human condition—extremes that also reveal extremes of disturbed relations.

Finally, I develop the concepts of mutual liberation and of the "loving fight." The nature of these must differ depending on which transactional modes have dominated the parent–child interactions. The final chapters also deal with the parents' disowned or impeded separation from their own parents and show how this burden from their past causes them to take their adolescent children to account for what their own parents did to them. This topic, finally, opens up the wider theme of psychological exploitation and liberation on which I shall elaborate in subsequent works.

ACKNOWLEDGMENTS

I gratefully acknowledge my debt to those members of our staff who, over the last six years, have cooperated in this study, particularly to Drs. Jack Baruch, Stephen G. Cronin, Joseph H. Herzberg, L. David Levi, Richard M. MacDonald,

Kent Ravenscroft, Jr., Robert J. Savard, Ms. Elizabeth Sherwood, and Mr. Stanley I. Hirsch, and to the members of the senior staff of the Adult Psychiatry Branch with whom I had many stimulating discussions: Drs. W. T. Carpenter, William Pollin, David Reiss, Winfield Scott, Roger Shapiro, John Strauss, and John Zinner. My special thanks go to Dr. Ivan Boszormenyi-Nagy who has alerted me to the importance of loyalty and other central family phenomena, and to Drs. Lyman Wynne and Margaret Singer and Ms. Kay Scheuer for their critique of the manuscript and their editing help. Finally, I thank Ms. Audrey Jordan for her unstinting secretarial assistance.

Helm Stierlin, M.D., Ph.D.

PART

I

1

A Dialectical Model of the Separation Process

Separation in adolescence is a transactional process between two parties—parents and children. This process can be a gradually expanding spiral of mutual individuation and differentiation occurring on various emotional, cognitive, and moral levels. Optimally, this spiraling leads to relative independence for both parties, yet is an independence based upon "mature *inter*dependence."

This ideal separation course does not, however, seem to be the rule. Rather, the transactions convey a sense of drama. Instead of a continuous saga, we see discontinuous episodes. Instead of expanding circular interactions, we notice disharmonious pulls and pushes between conflicting forces. Instead of gradual shifts and movements, either we see sudden reversals of positions and rapid changes of fortunes, or we observe periods of frozen stalemate.

Whether we note gradual differentiation or tumultuous drama depends, of course, on what a given adolescent and his family present to each other. But it also depends on our own vantage point and our conceptual framework for expressing what we see. This framework determines which data are selected and molded into meaningful and coherent patterns. The more elusive, complex, and interdependent the data, the more demands are made upon the conceptual framework to grasp them.

Here a conceptual model is offered to synthesize the elements of drama, the pushes and pulls, the sudden shifts in positions, in this transactional sequence of adolescent separation. This model is particularly suited to convey what goes on between those parents and adolescents who seek psychiatric help, but also applies to all other families.

This model was suggested by the philosophic writings of G. Hegel, especially by the famous chapter on "Master and Slave" in his *Phenomenology of the Spirit* (1806). Therein Hegel described the paradigm of a dyadic relationship between a dominant and a subordinate party—such as between jailer and prisoner, black man and white man, dominant male and subjugated female—in which the complex movements of partly complementary and partly conflictual psychological forces occur. These movements express a dialectical momentum. Shifts in positions are bound to occur, as a result of which the psychological composition of the relationship may change suddenly and dramatically. Each partner's contributions to, and satisfactions from, the relationship will be affected. For example, initially only the master in Hegel's paradigm seems to enjoy real satisfaction because he has leisure, while the drudging, exploited slave has none. Yet Hegel shows that the master's enjoyment of leisure becomes hollow to the extent that the slave saps his master's incentive for work. As a result, the master increasingly finds himself in the position of a bored playboy whose "pleasures" turn into the tedious killing of time. The slave, in contrast, although not free and forced to work, may learn to enjoy satisfactions of which his master knows nothing. For example, he may enjoy the rhythm of work and rest, or he may enjoy the struggle over a difficult task. A similar shift may occur in the balance of psychological dependency, and hence balance of power. At the outset, the master tends to appear independent and powerful and the slave totally dependent and powerless. Yet, as the relationship gets under way, the master becomes more dependent—and tends to strengthen the slave's psychological power over him, the master. This happened typically to many white masters in the American South who became increasingly dependent on their "powerful" house slaves (and also on their seemingly "weak and submissive" wives).

Such a dialectical concept of human transactions introduces a perspective that widens a traditional psychoanalytic view of object relations. Elsewhere I have dealt with the central elements of psychoanalytic object-relations theory (1970). This theory grew out of Freud's concept of instinctual drives in which drive satisfaction implied a response—or feedback—from others.* These others, or representatives of them, tended then to be conceptualized as objects.

To the extent that psychoanalytic theory grew more complex, different types of objects (e.g., inner and outer, part and whole, real and fantasized objects) emerged. At the same time, different types of relations between the subject and his objects and between these objects themselves came into focus. Thus, a complex interactional model began to take shape. This interactional model limited our perspective, however, because one (object-relating) individual and not the inter-

---

* Cf. Paul Ricoeur (1970): "The very notion of impulse or instinct, more basic than all the auxiliary representations of the topography, is distinct from the ordinary notion of instinct inasmuch as an instinct in the Freudian sense involves other persons. Hence, the final meaning of pleasure cannot be the discharge of tensions within an isolated apparatus; such a definition applies only to the solitary pleasure of autoerotic sexuality. Ever since the 'Project' Freud used the word 'satisfaction' (*Befriedigung*) for that quality of pleasure that requires the help of others" (p. 322).

action of several individuals (who relate to objects but also turn themselves into objects for others) remained the main locus of psychoanalytic inquiry.

The last decades have seen many attempts to overcome this limitation of psychoanalytic theory. The reasons are obvious to me: while our world contracted and became overcrowded, man's interdependence—with his fellow man (and with all living creatures)—became the overriding issue of the time. In order to survive, man had to become "interdependence-conscious." He had to develop an ecological awareness and this awareness had to shape psychoanalytic theory. The question then became: How could this happen?

While this question is debated in the analytic and popular literature (yet remains far from answered), competing transactional models have emerged. The most important of these is the systems model, inspired by modern notions of cybernetics.* This model has been applied to all social systems, particularly to families, and proved useful in many instances. For example, it allowed observers to see that symptoms such as depression may be "passed around" among different family members and yet remain within the closed system, that is, within the family. In balance, though, the systems model also is wanting. As yet, it provides too static and simplistic a view of human interactions. Many systems theorists omit the deeper levels of (mostly unconscious) guilt and obligation** which affect interpersonal systems, and they forget that living biological and social systems such as families are not closed, that they have components—i.e., individual members—who

---

* According to the *Oxford Dictionary of English Etymology*, "A theory of control in the animal or machine."

** Ivan Boszormenyi-Nagy (1972, 1973) is in my opinion the one author who has fully appreciated this deeper systems aspect of families.

6

change, grow, develop, and differentiate over time and who interact constantly with each other and with the outside world. Though having boundaries, these living systems are open to interchange and it is foremostly this interchange that needs to be grasped and described.

Such interchange is complex and it involves *movement, change, differentiation*, and *separation*. In order to do justice to these features, a dialectic relational approach is needed.

Here, I do not want to explain or deduce this approach in the abstract. How it works and what it can achieve must come across in the insights delivered in the chapters of this book.

Nonetheless, a few orienting remarks seem in order. In its original, general sense, the term *dialectic* refers to an investigation of truth by discussion. Thus understood, Plato's dialogues are exercises in the dialectic method, as are the *Critiques* of Kant. While this general meaning of dialectic still prevails in many philosophic quarters, we must also take into account how Hegel and Marx subsequently narrowed it. Hegel described a movement—i.e., the push, pull, and reconciliation—of ideas, whereas Marx, who stood Hegel on his head, declared such movement of ideas to be secondary to a movement of material, that is, socioeconomic forces. He derided Hegel for getting lost in the nebulous *superstructure* (*Überbau*), rather than studying the material base, on which Hegel's ideal superstructure rested. Not unlike Hegel and Marx, I present in the following the push and pull of partly conflicting, partly collusive forces; yet I am concerned neither with Marx's materialistic substructure nor with Hegel's idealistic superstructure. Rather, I focus on what H. Kilian (1971) has called the *middle-structure* (*Mittelbau*), which reflects the movement of those intrapsychic and interpersonal forces that somehow reside in between the two aforementioned structures. And within this middle realm, I am primarily concerned with one sector—that which includes parents and their adolescent children.

While this approach tends to highlight extreme movements and constellations, it also allows us to see the ordinary in perspective. The reader should keep in mind that most adolescent relations and separation processes, including those called "normal," fall somewhere in between the extremes that are the main topic of this book.

Finally, this dialectical approach reflects a basic methodological tension and ambiguity: it views the relating parties as active agents and contributors to the ongoing transactional process. *Their* (conscious and unconscious) intentions, *their* actions, *their* sufferings, *their* messages to, and perceptions of, the other are the main focuses of study. At the same time, it conceives of the transactional process as more than the sum of such contributions: it brings into view forces and patterns —or, if you wish, systemic properties—of the relationship which shape its course and reciprocally affect what the parties contribute.

This dialectical approach, when applied to the adolescent separation process, requires us to repeatedly change our investigative focus—e.g., from the adolescent to the parents, back to the adolescent, and so forth—while characteristic transactional dynamics emerge and are investigated. Thus, the very style of this presentation tries to convey the dynamic push and pull of the psychological forces that are its topic.

In this book I stress, above all, the contributions of the parents to the separation process—in contrast to a vast transactional and psychoanalytic literature wherein the children are described as the main initiators and agents of separation. Specifically, I want to indicate how parents contribute to the dialectical relational drama, how they affect, and are affected by, the push and pull of complex and conflicting forces. But such emphasis on the parents' contributions notwithstanding, we shall also examine the separating adolescent and begin our exposition by devoting the next chapter to him.

2

Running Away in the Context of Adolescent Separation

———

Runaways, I argued earlier, open up a perspective through which the separation process can be studied in depth. Here I want to develop this perspective: I want to show how adolescent runaways, the prodigal sons and daughters of today—as well as their nonrunaway counterparts—cast into relief what seems most central to adolescent separation. And I want to do so by focusing at first on the adolescents', as against the parents', contributions to the separation drama. As an initial step, I shall summarize some relevant features of adolescence.

According to the psychoanalytic viewpoint, the adolescent drives toward autonomy and identity by internalizing and tolerating conflicts and by actively seeking partners and values outside his or her family of origin. This drive is fueled and shaped by social expectations as well as by psychophysiological developments that affect the adolescent's total being. His aggressive and libidinal drives intensify, his defensive organization realigns, and his relational vicissitudes increase. A. Freud (1946), P. Blos (1962, 1970), E. Erikson (1950), and others have amply described these processes.

Additionally, adolescence ushers in the final maturation of

certain intellectual functions, of differentiated perceptions, and of moral capacities, chiefly during the thirteenth and fourteenth years. P. Inhelder and J. Piaget (1958), J. Adelson (1971), J. Kagan (1971), and L. Kohlberg and C. Gilligan (1971) have documented this period of intellectual maturation. As a result of such maturation, and a widening time perspective, the adolescent—for the first time in his life—can carry out complex reversible logical operations and can explore reflectively and imaginatively alternate actions and goals. At the same time, he enlarges his vocabulary of human motives and increases his grasp of psychological complexity. And he now experiences emotions as states of the self rather than as correlates of external events. Therefore, he can increasingly differentiate and clarify conflicting attitudes, intentions, needs, and motives within himself and, importantly, within others.*

Into this period fall also shifts and transformations of loyalty. Such shifts and transformations are relative. While he tries to remain loyal to his parents, the adolescent must yet move away from them and modify his parental introjects so that he can invest (or cathect) persons and values outside his family of origin in a relatively guilt-free manner. In this way, he finally "resolves" his "Oedipus complex."

These developments, intrinsic to the process of "adolescing," must be seen in juxtaposition to present-day American and Western society. This society, in the grip of unprecedented changes, affects on many levels how and whether the adolescent reaches autonomy.

Several aspects stand out here: Because its institutions, values, and identity-support structures are changing so rapidly,

---

* This holds true, in general. However, different adolescents seem to vary in the degree of their maturation of cognitive skills. D. Shainberg (1970) has made this point. Cf. also R. Shapiro (1968).

this society can less and less provide a stable anchorage and reference point for that which, in the words of Hegel, is "changing in and for itself"—namely, adolescence. Instead of offering such an anchorage, this society tolerates, or even institutionalizes, a volatile youth culture, often called the *counterculture*.

This youth culture promises and represents new life styles and values which conflict, albeit often ambiguously, with those held or professed by the parent generation. At the same time, it offers to many youngsters an alternative to living at home; that is, it turns into a temporary or lasting haven for early separators and runaways. The youth culture thus becomes a *"runaway culture."* The existence of this runaway culture affects many an adolescent's moves. Unlike the little child who remains dependently tied to his parents for good or bad, a modern-day adolescent can remove himself from his family and still expect to survive, particularly during the warm summer months. The question then becomes: Why and when does an adolescent opt to run away from home? In order to answer this question, we must first look at the runaway culture.

THE RUNAWAY CULTURE

This runaway culture owes much to special geographic and historical circumstances: e.g., a country with wide open expanses that invite roaming and exploration; easily available transportation, particularly cars and motorcycles; suburban wastelands whose barrenness contrasts with what the adolescent imagination seeks; mass media which make appear desirable, common, and feasible a Bohemian life that in previous times was hidden in metropolitan enclaves; a general affluence whose spillover guarantees survival even to the penniless;* and, finally, the existence of, and knowledge about, other runaways, their friends, and friends of friends—who by now constitute a large, informal, supportive network throughout the United States. These and other factors have given rise to a new—and, at the same time, old—nomadic life in the affluent jungle, a life that, while in many respects is cruelly harsh, promises romance, adventure, and freedom.

Still, the existence of a runaway culture alone ordinarily does not suffice to turn adolescents into runaways. In addition, we must assume a predisposition to run away and a painful and difficult home life from which the adolescent needs to escape. Yet, by the same token, we can speak of a predisposition to stay, i.e., *not* to run away—even though the home life seems unbearable and to run away would theoretically be feasible. This dual aspect of the modern runaway problem—that it bears on adolescents who do not run *and* those who do—causes us to reflect on the meaning of runaway success and failure.

RUNAWAY SUCCESS AND FAILURE

When I speak of runaway success, I have in mind youngsters who "succeed" merely in availing themselves of a pathological mode of separation which modern society offers its adolescents. Through running away, they escape their parents and make themselves prematurely independent. Yet such runaway

---

* The members of the Charles Manson household, all runaways, the majority being girls, lived, according to a *Life* magazine article, on food picked from garbage cans which they transformed into "delicious meals."

success—i.e., achievement of geographical distance and/or of premature independence—does not necessarily mean present or later success in life. The contrary is often true. Also, such "runaway success" is always a matter of degree. Runaways can stay away for hours, days, weeks, or months, and can achieve much or little geographical distance from their home and much or little premature autonomy.

Let us, then, keeping in mind the above qualifications, first turn to the "runaway failures."

Among these failures, we count, first, those adolescents who stay homebound even though their family life, to outward appearances, is difficult and miserable. While studying forty NIMH families of troubled adolescents over the last six years, I examined twelve such homebound adolescents side by side with twenty-eight others who had run away. The nonrunaways' family life seemed destructive; they seemed pained, and yet they stayed. Why? While pondering this question, I became alerted to a special subgroup of runaways whom I call "abortive runaways."

ABORTIVE RUNAWAYS

These abortive runaways, whom I include among the runaway failures, were not totally homebound. Occasionally they tried to run away precipitously, but never got off the ground, as it were. They were pulled back quickly, as if held on an invisible rubber leash. Either they returned home within hours, as if steered by an inner gyroscope, or they engineered their quick retrieval through the intervention of neighbors, police, or others. One fourteen-year-old boy, for example, repeatedly ran away; but only a few blocks away from his home he would loiter around a traffic crossing in such an absent-minded fashion that a policeman would become concerned. After domestic hassles another abortive runaway, a girl of about the same age, would run angrily into a park, yet leave her bicycle in sight of neighbors who were friends of her parents. The very abortiveness and ambivalence of these adolescents' runaway attempts highlighted their strong, intact psychological ties to their families.

LONELY SCHIZOID RUNAWAYS

Among the group of abortive runaways, I found subsequently most of those runaways whom I have come to call "lonely schizoid runaways." These lonely schizoid runaways differ from most other runaways. Their relations to the runaway culture are marginal, at best. Ordinarily, they have no peers to run to. They may loiter around hippie hangouts, or may even prefer lonely parks and churchyards. In running away, they seem lured by idiosyncratic introjects, not by living people. Not seldom are their runaway moves abruptly aborted. One girl in this group ran to the next street corner where she froze in panic. The panic lifted when a policeman took her by the hand and led her home. Other lonely schizoid runaways act so bizarrely or self-destructively that they are quickly institutionalized. One such runaway boy was Roy.

Roy entered our outpatient treatment program at the age of sixteen, together with his parents and his younger brother, Bill. One year before, Roy had begun to be late for school, and occasionally had skipped his classes altogether. His alarmed and tense mother had arranged for Roy to see a psychiatrist twice a week. Roy, however, had shown no more enthusiasm for his psychotherapy than he had shown for his schoolwork. He was tardy in attending his therapy sessions and eventually rejected them altogether.

In the family sessions he was mostly mute. Sometimes he wore a whimsical smile on his face; more often he seemed sullen. A number of times he exploded and devastated his mother with some perceptive and unfavorable comment on her behavior or motives. He attended the family sessions irregularly and finally dropped out completely. His parents then continued for a while with couple sessions. A few months later these couple sessions also came to an end as the mother wanted to return to her former psychiatrist. By this time Roy had lost all interest in school. He spent almost all his time alone in his room, either reading, tinkering with stereo equipment, or just staring in front of himself. He refused to meet his former buddies and made no attempts to get to know girls. A few times, however, he deigned to receive and go out with one former classmate.

After roaming the streets with this boy one particular evening, Roy did not return home as expected. Instead, he continued to wander around in the city after his friend had left him. Night descended, but he roamed around until the early morning hours, when he climbed on a fire-escape ladder into a fifth-floor apartment in a big residential building. Here he stumbled into a sleeping young woman who alerted the police. The police, after checking with his parents, delivered Roy to a nearby psychiatric institution. Here he remained hospitalized for several months. He was then transferred to a residential-treatment center for adolescents with school problems, from which he repeatedly ran away. Roy, then nineteen, has spent the last year in a psychiatric hospital, diagnosed as schizophrenic. By now he has run away from this hospital a dozen or so times.

CASUAL RUNAWAYS

In contrast to homebound and abortive runaways, many successful runaways seem to experience neither qualms nor difficulties when they separate from their families. Nor do they seem blocked from moving into the runaway culture of peers. Rather than appearing agonized and labile, they impress us as casual and tough. Hence, I have come to speak of "casual runaways."

Unlike lonely schizoid runaways, who seem terrified of most peer and particularly (if they are boys) girl relations, these "casual runaways," or, better, "driftaways," easily find girls who turn into willing sex partners. Yet, too, they discard these girls casually once they have used them. Their object relations are typically transient, shallow, and exploitative and, being ruthless and tough, they seem well equipped to survive in the rougher segments of the runaway culture. George belonged to this group.

As a small child George was difficult to handle. His parents said he did only what he wanted to, never heeding their warnings or limits. When his parents tried to control him, he threw temper tantrums and became obnoxious. In the end they always let him have his way for the sake of peace. Also, from early on, George showed a "tough and mean" side. He extorted other children's money by threatening to smash their heads, stole their food, and seemed bent on mischief. He often ran away from home, first for hours, then for half days, then for days. He ran away for several days at the age of fourteen after he had stolen some jewelry out of his mother's jewelry chest and she had found out. He returned after he had gambled away the money and had heard his father insist on the telephone that his mother would die of a heart attack should he stay away longer. During the three months of outpatient therapy with his family, George ran away from home once and missed several sessions "because he had something important to do." The "something important," I learned later, were his activities in a tough motorcycle gang. During the year and a half since family therapy ended, George has completely dropped out of school. He did not show up for a follow-up interview, and his parents stated that "he is at home sometimes and sometimes not." The last I heard about him was that he had been arrested for participating in a burglary that netted the gang several thousand dollars' worth of jewelry.

CRISIS RUNAWAYS

In between unsuccessful nonrunaways and abortive runaways, on the one side, and successful casual runaways, on the other, we find those numerous runaways of "medium or qualified success" who, in varying measure, contain elements of both patterns (i.e., the "abortive runaway" *and* the "driftaway" patterns). Here belongs the boy or girl who runs away for a few days or even weeks before he or she returns home (or, more frequently, is forced to return home). The runaway scenario can vary. A fifteen-year-old boy, for example, planned for weeks to join his friends at an ocean resort in case the going with his parents should remain rough. Predictably, it remained rough, and so he ran. However, despite his planning, he forgot his bathing trunks and the money he had saved. He realized these oversights only when he arrived at the beach. While there, he could not help making himself conspicuous near the cottage of family friends who spotted him and informed his parents. Runaway girls of this group soon become promiscuous or even pregnant and thereby confirm their parents' worst apprehensions. Yet, too, more or less covertly, they make sure thereby that their parents rescue them and "straighten out their mess." These runaways can be called partly successful because they get away from their parents for longer stretches of time than the abortive runaways and, unlike the latter, can find a niche in the runaway culture of peers. And, for a while at least, they can make it on their own (providing, of course, there is spillover from society's affluence). Yet, unlike most casual runaways, they remain involved with their families, often intensely so, and finally return to the family orbit. While away from home (yet still on a leash), they often seem deeply conflicted—conflicted about running away from their parents, about living in the runaway culture, about hurting others while pursuing their own ends. Above all, their running away reflects a crisis in their and their parents' lives. Consequently, I have come to speak of them as "crisis runaways." Such a crisis runaway is Lorraine.

Up to the age of fifteen, Lorraine did well in school and gave no reason for concern. Suddenly, though, everything went wrong and she ran away from home overnight. Her parents learned from the police the next morning that she had been picked up in an abandoned house together with several young persons who had LSD and marijuana in their pockets. Lorraine received stern warnings from all sides—parents, police, teachers—and refrained from running away for a while. Yet things did not go well for her. She slept around with several boys, took drugs in varying amounts, and skipped many classes. In order to conceal her truancy from school, she forged passes and lied to anybody and everybody. Finally the bubble burst. She saw herself in an inextricable mess, suffocating under the web of lies she had spun, disgusted with herself because of her promiscuity and drug abuse. She ran away from home to a hippie commune in a northern metropolis. Two and a half days later her father retrieved her from there. Lorraine returned home tired, hungry, unwashed, disillusioned, and ready for anything, including family therapy. Almost at the onset of this therapy she began to "find herself." She again became a good student and seemed to abstain from mischief. The subsequent individual therapy revealed that her situation was not quite as rosy as Lorraine had made it appear to her parents and therapist. She still used drugs occasionally, carried on sexually with two boys, and participated in some orgies. By the end of her individual therapy, however, her progress seemed more solid. Most importantly, she had begun to become aware of some neurotic anxieties and conflicts that had prompted her delinquent and runaway behavior. She began to reflect on her low self-esteem, her "unnatural sexual cravings," and her fear of men, marriage, and babies—all matters she had tried to push out of her mind by counterphobically dashing into promiscuity and drugs. After a period of moderate depression, Lorraine began to shift gears as far as her major activities and relationships were concerned. She involved herself in school clubs, became editor of her school newspaper, and learned a foreign language. When one day she noticed high-school students younger than herself taking LSD and "fooling around with needles" in a back corner of the schoolyard, this struck her as a bad dream of the kind she herself had left behind. She has not run away again and is now successfully enrolled in college.

Although Lorraine's troubles appeared at times serious and comparable to those of George, a closer acquaintance with her and her family left no doubt that she belonged to a different group than George. Her troubles predominantly reflected a crisis that began when she was fifteen. A number of factors came together to make this crisis relatively traumatic and long-lasting. Among them were the activation of guilt feelings and conflicts thriving on the intense upsurge of her sexual and aggressive drives; the availability of a deviant peer group with a reputation for adventurous mischief (orgies, smoking pot, and taking LSD); and, perhaps most important, two parents who at that time could not help burdening her with problems of their own. Presently, Lorraine—immersed in studies, poetry, and college activities—seems to have mastered her crisis.

How can we grasp the forces that pull adolescents away from, or draw them to, their families? Clearly, these forces reside partly in the adolescent, partly in the parents and families, and partly in the relationship that holds together *and* pushes apart the generations.

In order to understand these forces better and, at the same time, to understand why certain adolescents do or do not run away while still others run away abortively, we must next consider broadly the parents' roles in the separation process.

3

Modern Middle-Aged Parents

Compared to the attention that adolescents receive in the literature, their parents until now have remained neglected. For example, comprehensive works on the life cycle—such as those of E. Erikson (1959) and T. Lidz (1968)—only sparsely or belatedly deal with the problems of middle-aged parents. This is understandable as their life phase, compared to that of their children, offers few landmarks or critical turning points worth investigating. Yet, as we shall see, such relative neglect of parents is unwarranted.

I shall analyze the parents' positions and their contributions to the separation process by focusing on those features which I have earlier mentioned as most essential in adolescent development: the *intensification of drives, the growth of cognitive skills, the shift of loyalties,* and *the existence of a runaway culture.* In parents, these features reflect developmental trends that mostly run counter to what we find in adolescence and hence highlight differences between parents and children. This approach, inevitably, leaves out and condenses much that is important in the lives of middle-aged parents. It is a first attempt to map out central aspects of a life phase that is essentially uncharted. In particular, it neglects to bring into view many important tasks and substages of this life phase as these apply differently to men and women. These limitations notwithstanding, the earlier-mentioned features of adolescence stake out the investigation that follows. For not only are these features central to adolescent development, they also reveal the major themes in the parents' lives by the time their adolescent children separate. In focusing on each of these features, we become alerted to critical issues which embroil the parents in conflicts and which require reconciliation or resignation.

All these issues reflect a mid-life crisis which stirs because death draws closer. "The paradox," writes E. Jaques (1965), "is that of entering the prime of life, the stage of fulfillment, but at the same time the prime and fulfillment are dated. Death lies beyond . . . this fact . . . is the central and crucial feature of the mid-life phase . . ." (p. 506). All that one has done and still can do needs to be assessed in the light of this fact. Such needed assessment can tax us to the utmost as it seems to have taxed Dante when, at the age of thirty-seven, he began *The Divine Comedy* with these stanzas:

In the middle of the journey of our life, I came to myself within a dark wood where the straight way was lost. Ah, how hard it is to tell of that wood, savage and harsh and dense, the thought of which renews my fear. So bitter is it that death is hardly more.

Like E. Jaques, I interpret this as the opening scene of a vivid and perfect description of the emotional crisis of the mid-life phase (1965).

PARENTAL DRIVES COMPARED WITH ADOLESCENT DRIVES

As a rule, the parents of adolescents are over age forty. They are established in society, and often wield power, but their life curve is descending while that of their children is ascending. While aggressive and libidinal drives are awakening in their children, these parents feel the decline of such drives. For example, regarding their libidinal drives, they may conclude, as did Proust's Swann (in the first volume of A la Recherche du Temps Perdu), that in this phase of life love has set its tracks; "it no longer unfolds spontaneously according to its unknown laws in a heart wondrously awed and captivated. Now we tinker with it, we push and distort it with the help of memory and suggestion. When we recognize one of its symptoms, we remember others and thus give love a new lease." This decline of drives holds true despite wide individual variations in energy levels and preserved youthfulness, and despite or because of frequent erotic and aggressive dashes during this life phase.

These dashes can be rightful vitalizing moves designed to enrich and enliven the middle-aged person's one and only life. But also, they may be mere counterphobic proof that the person still has intact potency and vigor when his (or her) actual situation and appearance tell otherwise. When these dashes are last-ditch efforts to capture (or recapture) a fading youth, the awakening can be rude and the task of accepting one's declining life course and strength even more painful. The aging Professor Rath, in the film The Blue Angel, exemplifies the tragic foolishness of erotic flings in middle age when one's developmental phase and station in life seem to require other behavior.

Often it is difficult to decide—for the outsider as well as for the middle-aged parent—whether outbursts of passion in middle age serve the person's growth or his self-deception, whether they represent legitimate energizing moves, or are foolish, self-deceiving ventures. Therefore, they are likely to become matters for doubt and inner conflict.

Such conflict in middle-aged persons—who, when engaging in amorous or aggressive ventures, may court self-deception, disillusionment, and final rejection or who, in foregoing such ventures, may opt for premature closure and resignation—sharpens when these persons sense in themselves a backlog of an unlived life and, especially, an unlived adolescence. In this case, the attempt to give counterphobic proof of one's (inwardly doubted) remaining vitality can merge with the desperate and self-blinding wish to find passion and fulfillment when none can be had. This is conveyed, for example, in Thomas Mann's novel, *The Black Swan*, written at the time when Mann was far into middle age.

PARENTAL SKILLS COMPARED WITH ADOLESCENT SKILLS

Adolescence, we saw in the preceding chapter, ushers in and consolidates the individual's final cognitive growth. In middle-aged parents we find no comparable cognitive development. In most individuals of age thirty or older, the IQ tests slowly begin to show poorer results, comparing unfavorably with what these persons scored at the peak of their adolescence. Also, as adults, their "moral growth," i.e., their grasp of moral complexities—which in large part presupposes a lively, questioning intelligence—tends to become arrested and their moral sensibility declines, indeed, often regresses to a level below that which they had achieved at the height of their adolescence. This finding was suggested by Piaget in 1932 and was recently confirmed by Kohlberg and Gilligan (1971).

If parents are lucky, they derive comfort from having used well what they built up and learned in *their* adolescence, especially if they have articulated, consolidated, and enjoyed their mastery of the world. But frequently the skills learned in adolescence have lost some of their promise and luster. Often they are blunted from too much routine usage. Although the extent of such "blunting" of alertness and inquisitiveness varies from one middle-aged individual to another and new learning and cognitive ventures are possible throughout one's adult life, such ventures appear more difficult and cumbersome now than they seemed in adolescence.

The decline of the cognitive skills and of the intellectual curiosity of middle-aged parents is hastened when these parents are stuck in marital or professional dead ends, as is the lot of many parents in present-day American society. Until recently, this society has fostered marital dead ends, particularly for women, by putting a premium on early marriage and married life in general—in contrast to sectors of the European society with which I am familiar. Thus, instead of granting to young adults the time and study opportunities needed to ingrain and stimulate intellectual interests, this society, through the power of its shared values and expectations, corrals its young men and women into early marital havens that often mean the end of their intellectual growth. This is most evident in the case of many women, but also holds true for men who, in order to become early providers for their families, often cut short the moratorium of adolescence (as described by E. Erikson) and accept jobs that are intrinsically boring and lacking in opportunities.

In restricting their intellectual and moral horizons as young adults, these parents have laid the ground for the experience of deep hurt, pain, or silent despair in their middle age, when they realize that because of what they failed to do earlier—namely, branch out intellectually when it was the best time to do so—their options and competitive postures in life have shrunk. Also here we find then the need to come to grips with one's limitations and missed opportunities while challenges still abound.

This makes understandable some of the overt and covert despair and depression we find in middle-aged parents, and, also, the frequently urgent wish for new beginnings that many of them feel, which is a topic that will occupy us next.

LOYALTY AND THE QUEST FOR NEW BEGINNINGS

Adolescents, we found, need to modify and partly shift loyalties away from their family of origin toward persons and values outside this family. Middle-aged parents, in contrast, seem, above all, to need to assess and confirm *existing loyalties*. They ask themselves whether they have fulfilled commitments and carried out their responsibilities as parents to their children, as children to their own parents, as professionals, and as members of the community. All this seems part of the quest for integrity which Erikson (1959) believes characterizes this life phase. K. Jaspers, thinking along similar lines, emphasized the need for a *"lebensentscheidende Treue,"* a fidelity that determines one's life. Further, such a quest for integrity and fidelity seems to imply a strong recognition of spiritual and religious values. C. G. Jung, more than most other psychologists concerned with the problems of middle-aged individuals, has especially emphasized the need for such recognition once life has passed its halfway mark (after age forty). And even though the contents of traditional religions become questionable to many—because these contents are challenged through scientific exegesis and are relativized through the heightened awareness of other creeds—the religious urge gains strength; an urge that reflects the original meaning of *re-ligare* (as, for example, employed by Servius, Lactantius, and Augustine): *to bind fast, to tie to one's roots, to be loyal.* Along with the affirmation of existing loyalties and commitments, a more contemplative attitude toward life and the world seems required as one moves inexorably toward death.

Such affirmation of commitments and existing loyalties, however, often conflicts with what we may call the commitment to one's growth: the urge and need to realize one's full potentials, to test out one's limits, to open one's self to new experiences, challenges, and relations. Parents in middle age ask themselves not only whether they have fulfilled commitments, but also whether they have lived up to the promises of their youth. Viewed from this vantage point, it is understandable that Dr. Robert Butler, a noted authority on problems of aging and the life cycle, extolls the value of ever-repeated identity crises for middle-aged people (1973). Such identity crises, which often imply intrapsychic and interpersonal upset, are the subjective correlates of the new beginnings that seem required.*

The conflict of middle-aged parents over whether they should honor and deepen existing loyalties, or whether they should embark on new beginnings, becomes more intense when the surrounding society not only tolerates and justifies such new beginnings, but also provides opportunities for their realization. And this, to an unprecedented extent, is the case in our present American society.

* Cf. S. Lessard, 1971, and *Time*, August 3, 1970.

A RUNAWAY CULTURE FOR MIDDLE-AGED ADULTS

In order to understand the lure and feasibility of new beginnings for middle-aged adults, we can draw a parallel to the youth culture of early separators which I have described as a runaway culture. For the changes in today's American society that give rise to the phenomenon of the runaway culture have also, though less ostensibly, created a new "scene" for adults. More easily than was possible before, this societal scene provides opportunities for new learning, new relationships, new jobs—in brief, new beginnings. The women's liberation movement, which has gained momentum during the last few years, illustrates this trend. It alerts women to new types of experiences, jobs, and identities (as reflected in the adoption of the more self-assertive Ms. as against Miss or Mrs.) which, in one way or the other, imply a realignment of, or breakaway from, existing living patterns and loyalties.

And while making more easily available and legitimate new jobs, identities, and life styles, this society, at the same time, makes the exit from established jobs and institutions easier. Marriages, in particular, can be ended more easily or—with society's overt or covert permission—can be sidestepped or supplanted by other living arrangements such as communal forms of living and trial or common-law marriages.

Wanda Lee Adams from Seattle, Washington, described as a "dropout wife" in *Life* magazine (March 17, 1972), is one middle-aged woman (though, at thirty-five, still on the young side of middle age) who made a new beginning. One evening, according to *Life*,

Wanda Lee Adams, college graduate, wife of a middle-level Seattle executive and mother of three, walked out on her family to begin a new life on her own. There was no great animosity then, nor is there now. No dramatic grievances existed, and by most standards the 14-year marriage was a success. Her husband Don was considerate, attentive and devoted. Money was not a factor. The problem was that somewhere around her tenth year of marriage, Wanda Adams had begun to see her life as increasingly frustrating and suffocating. She started to work again and enjoyed it. She went back to school and there encountered the women's liberation movement. "I then realized," she says, "that I was experiencing what a lot of women experience. Don was a decent human being who had allowed me to grow to a certain point. But past that point I had to leave."

And she did.

"The breakup of a home for such cool reasons," the *Life* article continues,

is no longer rare. No accurate statistics exist, but around the country, interviews with marriage counselors, psychiatrists, detective agencies—as well as women's liberation groups—confirm the growth of what is called the phenomenon of the dropout wife. Most dropouts are middle-class, educated, highly motivated women who have been married a number of years. Some, but by no means all, are also women's liberation converts like Wanda Lee Adams.

In brief, just as the newly emerging youth culture is critically influencing the developmental course of modern adolescents, the widespread emergence of "new life opportunities" coupled with a new permissiveness cannot but influence the developmental course of their parents. These parents, too, may feel tempted to move away or run away from jobs and family relations which, they believe, only mire them in stalemates and hassles. They, too, may desperately wish to make new starts in life and, like their adolescent children, may strongly feel the lure of a "runaway culture."

This, then, introduces a further source of conflict into their lives. For when the "runaway tendencies" of parents are activated, they run counter to at least some of those developmental trends and tasks outlined earlier, which foremostly imply the acceptance and confirmation of existing relations and commitments. Thus, these tendencies are bound to further embroil the parents in conflict and to make more difficult the needed task of reconciliation.

CENTRIPETAL VERSUS CENTRIFUGAL CONFLICT SOLUTIONS FOR COUPLES

The middle-age crises that parents experience as individuals reverberate into their relationship as couples. Many levels of this relationship are affected. The concepts of *centripetal* and *centrifugal* forces reveal typical ways in which this may happen. I employed these concepts originally when I described separation patterns between the generations, which will be the topic of the next chapter. Here, I shall apply the concepts to couples only.

Typically, the above conflicts and tasks of reconciliation can push a couple toward either a more centrifugal or more centripetal "solution." This, then, accounts for two ideal–typical patterns of middle-aged couple relationships which form the extremes on a scale that also allows for various in-between states. In my clinical practice with couples and families, I have found it increasingly useful and easy to place middle-aged parents on this scale.

Mr. and Mrs. Franklin, for example, represent a "centripetal couple." They are in their mid-forties; their looks betray strain, fatigue, and subdued irritation with each other.

But in the presence of a psychiatrist they try eagerly to correct any impression that anything is wrong with their marriage. They hold hands, smile at each other endearingly, and emphasize that there is basically no problem between them. (Their only "real" problem rests in the child for whom they seek help!) To them, any thought of separation or divorce seems inappropriate and, in fact, inconceivable. (Somehow Mr. and Mrs. Franklin forget to mention—or push out of their minds —that their sex life dried up over the last few years. But this fact, in their opinion unnecessarily unearthed by the psychiatrist, according to them does not reflect lack of love for, or interest in, each other; rather, it is due to Mrs. Franklin's migraine headaches, which happen to overcome her at bedtime. Also, they admit after a while, it is perhaps due to Mr. Franklin's having become unduly fatigued by his heavy professional duties and worries over his child.)

In Mr. and Mrs. Franklin we notice a pseudomutual style of relating, as described by L. Wynne, et al. (1958), and documented by M. Singer and L. Wynne (1966) in the Rorschach productions of these parents. Where this relational style prevails, the partners express only positive, good, harmonious, loving feelings toward each other and keep dissociated, and fail to express, negative, angry, and hostile ones, even though a perceptive observer may detect such feelings. We find, in brief, a rose-colored togetherness whose squelching and divisive undercurrents are denied or shut out by the partners. Paradoxically, as L. Wynne has further shown (1965), a squelching togetherness also may exist in couples where the divisive undercurrents take the center stage—i.e., where anger and frustration are expressed openly and constantly—while loving and tender feelings recede into dissociation. In these cases, Wynne spoke of pseudohostility, which he considers structurally akin to pseudomutuality.

From the vantage point adopted here, both pseudomutuality and pseudohostility represent attempts at centripetal conflict solutions. In both instances those forces dominate that seek to contain potentially disruptive drives, that is, forces which work counter to new experiences outside the marriage and which support the relational status quo. Whatever inner conflicts have been stirred up in these middle-aged parents, these conflicts appear somehow controlled by a commitment to continuous marital togetherness, restrictive and precarious as this may be. Particularly pseudohostile couples seem instructive. Despite the fact that they cannot help lapsing into bitter fights wherever they are (with an unknown psychiatrist they usually resume their fights within minutes), they cannot seriously consider separation or divorce. They seem no less insolubly tied to each other than are the "loving" pseudomutual pairs.

Extremes of centrifugal conflict solutions in middle-aged couples are more difficult to delineate than centripetal solutions. For a centrifugal solution, when radical, implies the dissolution of the marriage—the spouses separate or divorce. This, then, leaves the observer with the task of conducting a postmortem on a dead relationship rather than assessing one that is still alive. Here, I want to focus on couple relationships that still show some life even though they are beset by strong centrifugal forces. Among these relationships is that of Mr. and Mrs. Dixon.

In contrast to Mr. and Mrs. Franklin, Mr. and Mrs. Dixon had no difficulty admitting that their marriage was difficult, problem ridden, and stormy. In fact, for a number of years it had been (nearly) on the rocks. There had been innumerable bitter mutual accusations about who had caused this result. But these accusations did not reflect the spirit of a pseudohostility that would imply an ongoing, closely knit, though unharmonious, togetherness. Instead, Mr. and Mrs. Dixon came to go more and more their own ways, i.e., they increasingly learned to seek and find satisfactions outside their marital relationship. Both spouses had a string of extramarital affairs and both embarked on new careers that were pulling them in different directions. However, despite the dominance of centrifugal forces in their marriage, they had as yet not broken up completely. They said they could not do this because their children still needed them.

In whatever way middle-aged parents seek to solve the problems of their life phase—be this in a more centripetal or more centrifugal fashion—any such solution, most likely, will be precarious or problematical as the underlying conflicts and ambivalences remain. It is at this point in our investigation, where we have surveyed the problems of middle-aged parents but have detected no easy solutions, that we must turn to the perhaps most important factor in their situation—their children, who by now are adolescents and push for their separation. Given this factor, these parents cannot but make their children party to their own drama just as these children, on their parts, cannot help involving their parents in their drama. Thus, there opens up to us a scenario wherein the distinct developmental conflicts and problems of parents, as well as those of their children, fatefully overlap and intermesh.

4

Centripetal and Centrifugal Forces in the Adolescent Separation Drama

To grasp the drama of separating parents and children, I developed the concept of *transactional modes*. These modes reflect the interplay and/or relative dominance of centripetal and centrifugal pushes *between the generations*, rather than those between marital partners, as described in the foregoing chapter. In the intergenerational interplay, the transactional modes operate as the covert organizing transactional background to the more overt and specific child–parent interactions.* When age-appropriate transactional modes are out of phase, too intense, or inappropriately mixed with other modes, the negotiation of a mutual individuation and separation between parent and child is impeded.

The transactional modes reflect salient contributions of the parents and of the children to the interpersonal process. The modes are *transitive and reciprocal. They are transitive* in that they denote the active molding of an offspring who is still

* I am indebted to Dr. K. Ravenscroft, Jr., for this formulation.

immature, dependent, and hence remains captive to parental influences. This accords with the fact that parents, from the beginning, impress on their child their "stronger reality" (Stierlin, 1959). They do this often unconsciously by using covert and subtle signals and sanctions. To this "stronger reality" a child must adapt lest he perish. Additionally, *these modes are reciprocal* in the sense that there is always a two-way exchange. In this exchange, the children mold and influence their parents as much as the latter mold and influence them.

We can distinguish between the three major modes of *binding, delegating,* and *expelling.* As I shall try to show, all these modes reflect how adolescents do or do not run away. Table 1 may serve as a guide to the exposition that follows.

THE MODE OF BINDING

When this mode dominates, the family is gripped by centripetal forces. Parents and children operate under the unspoken assumption that essential satisfactions and securities can be obtained only within the family, while the outside world looks hostile and forbidding. This assumption then resonates in the attitudes of parents who, when faced with *their* developmental crisis, see only one avenue open to them: to tie their children ever more closely to themselves and to the "family ghetto" and to delay or prevent the children's separation at all cost.

While examining the runaway or nonrunaway status of my troubled adolescents, I saw binding chiefly in those disturbed

TABLE 1

Transactional Modes

(Transitive and Reciprocal)

CENTRIPETAL FORCES DOMINANT	CENTRIPETAL AND CENTRIFUGAL FORCES STRONG	CENTRIFUGAL FORCES DOMINANT
Reflected mainly in nonrunaways and certain abortive runaways, including lonely schizoid runaways	Reflected mainly in crisis runaways	Reflected mainly in casual runaways
A. BINDING	**B. DELEGATING**	**C. EXPELLING**
1st Level: Affective Binding (Id Binding) Exploitation mainly of dependency needs with emphasis on regressive gratification. (Infantilization of adolescent.) 2nd Level: Cognitive Binding (Ego Binding) Interference with differentiated self-awareness and self-determination. Mystification; violation of cognitive integrity; injection and/or withholding of meaning. 3rd Level: Binding Through the Exploitation of Loyalty (Superego Binding) Excessive breakaway guilt instilled; children turned into lifelong, self-sacrificing victim-adjuncts.	Adolescent sent out yet held back by "long leash of loyalty." A limited and qualified autonomy is allowed or encouraged, depending on which mission the delegate is expected to fulfill. Missions can be classified according to how they serve the parent's id, ego, or superego primarily. (Cf. Table 2.)	Enduring neglect and/or rejection of children who are pushed into premature and foreclosing autonomy. Weak loyalty bonds.

adolescents who *did not* run away or who ran away abortively. The very abortiveness of their runaway attempts clarified what was involved in binding.

The nonrunaways and abortive runaways shared one feature—*they tended to avoid peers.* This resulted from three interrelated factors: (1) they showed little or no drive to seek out and invest themselves in peers; (2) they feared excessively being "unmasked," being ridiculed, or being beaten up by peers; and (3) they lacked many of the relational skills needed to survive in a peer group.

I then looked more closely at this group of troubled nonrunaways and abortive runaways and their families, and reflected on the transactional dynamics involved in such avoidance of peers. As a result, I came to distinguish three (more or less interrelated) levels on which the binding mode operates: There is a first "affective" level on which the parent exploits his children's needs for elementary satisfaction and dependency; this I term "id binding." A second level exists on which mainly "cognitive processes" are involved; this I label "ego binding." And at a third level the child's loyalty is exploited; I call this "superego binding."

On each level the parents provide transactional nutriment inappropriate to their adolescent's age and needs.

Affective Binding

On the first—need-satisfying and affective—level, the parent infantalizes his (or her) child by offering undue regressive gratification. The motives for such parental action vary. An overgratifying parent may need to be confirmed as being giving and bountiful by a continuously dependent adolescent. Or such a parent may unconsciously need to repair past losses and deprivations which he or she suffered. Here we typically find a mother who tries to give her child all the love she herself missed as a child. In order to make up through active mastery for what she had once to endure passively, namely, deprivation and abuse, she now recruits her child and gives to him as she had needed to be given to. The more compelling her need for reparative gratification, the more likely she becomes an intrusive and indulging juggernaut, unable to see what the child needs in his own right. Her child cannot help becoming deprived and psychologically exploited in the very process of the mother's giving.

Further, a parent, by offering infantile gratifications, may try to forestall and subdue the adolescent's maturing sexuality which threatens him (or her) directly or indirectly—directly because it stirs up frightening incestuous desires; indirectly because it threatens to shatter his precarious equilibrium of sexual wishes, fears, and inhibitions.

Still further, by regressively gratifying offspring, a parent may try to cope with ambivalent, hostile, and rejecting impulses toward the child. The child serves as a living proof of his parent's lovingness. Such a child is exploited insofar as he is not allowed to experience and define his parent's feelings and motivations for what they are: hostile and rejecting.

Whatever the specific motivations that impel parents to bind their child, the stage is now set for a particular developmental drama. Its major force is the awakening of the child's libidinal and aggressive drives during adolescence. Under these circumstances, the parent cannot but contribute to dangerously reactivated preoedipal and oedipal conflicts. Because the child's awakened drives have no other objects, the parents (particularly the opposite sex parent) become the target of renewed symbiotic and/or incestuous pulls, replete with anxieties and conflicts. Short of engaging in murderous battles and actual incest, the binding parent must attempt to either divert or subdue the child's awakened libidinal and aggressive drives. If he (or she) manages to divert them away from himself, he will, in fact, loosen the bind. If not, he will have a tiger on his hands. Whether the interaction revolves around relatively harmless, "pregenital" activities such as eating, arguing, swearing, etc., or whether it is more openly sexual and sadomasochistic, heightened conflict (overt or covert) is inevitable. The more a binding mother gratifies, indulges, and spoils her child, the more insatiable and monsterlike the child becomes.

This dynamic interchange explains some of the features of the group of disturbed nonrunaways and abortive runaways. It suggests why some of these adolescents actually run away, yet return home quickly. They cannot find any peer or other adult who accepts their excessive demands for regressive gratification. Some of these adolescents resort to drugs with the covert encouragement of one or both parents. Drugs seem to offer the easiest way out of the aforementioned dilemma, because they curb the intensified libidinal and aggressive drives, and lessen the dilemma at least for a while.

I was impressed with how spoiled, infantile, and demanding this subgroup of adolescents appeared. One girl threatened her mother with a knife when the latter refused to drive her somewhere. A son in this group, according to his doting mother, had "the table manners of a disgusting cannibal," and unendingly showered her with four-letter words for not sufficiently attending to him, relishing his oral onslaughts.

Two other adolescents in this group had long histories of unspecified somatic complaints or illnesses such as low-grade fever and stomach pains. Both girls had frequent hospitalizations and diagnostic work-ups. Much of the family interaction centered around these illnesses and symptoms, accompanied by underlying rage, suffocating clinging, demands for nurturance, and manipulation by guilt. The illnesses and symptoms promised "legitimate regressive gratification" in a transactional setting that had become agonizing to both the parents and children. I was tempted to think of these somatizations as runaway equivalents.*

Binding on the Cognitive Level

A second binding mode operates on a cognitive rather than an affective level. When this happens, the binding parent interferes with his child's differentiated self-awareness and self-determination. The ability to perceive and articulate one's own feelings, needs, motives, and goals as against those that others attribute to oneself is crucial in order for the child to cope with any conflicts over his separation. Therefore, his parents' cognitive binding stratagems reduce his chances to master such conflicts.

H. Bruch, among others, described the paradigm of a cognitively binding parent (1961, 1962, 1966). She noted that a mother, by being intrusively interpretative, prevents her child from perceiving and differentiating his basic bodily needs or states such as hunger, thirst, or fatigue. She cognitively binds her child when she imposes on him her own definition of his

---

* Binding on the affective level, as described here, relates to the psychoanalytic concept of fixation. In defining this concept, O. Fenichel (1945) suggested intertwining transactional and intrapsychic dynamics. Transactionally, fixations (of drives) denote a history of either excessive gratification, excessive frustration, or abrupt alternations between both modes. Intrapsychically, "fixations are rooted in experiences of instinctual satisfaction which simultaneously gave reassurance in the face of some anxiety or aided in repressing some feared impulse. Such simultaneous satisfaction of drive and of security is the most common cause of fixations" (p. 66). The concept of binding can be seen as explicating the ongoing transactional dynamics which either sustain or give rise to such fixations.

feelings, needs, or intentions; thereby she substitutes her own for the child's regulatory and discriminating ego. She misdefines the child to himself. Such cognitive binding operates also when a mother trains her child to perceive her as loving, whereas in reality she is hostile, rejecting, or at least ambivalent. Also, a mother will very likely resort to cognitive binding when she must justify her own failure in life by depicting herself as victimized by overpoweringly bad and persecuting outside forces, a view which her child needs to share and confirm. The child's ego is deformed in the process. As a result of such maneuvers, the child is mystified about what he feels, needs, and wants. G. Bateson (1969), G. Bateson et al. (1956, 1963), L. Wynne (1963a, b), M. Singer (1965a, b), J. Haley (1959), and R. Laing (1965), among others, have elucidated various aspects of this transaction.

I am inclined to call cognitive binding "ego binding," as the binder forces the bindee to rely on the binder's distorted and distorting ego instead of using and developing his own discriminating ego.

Cognitive—or "ego"—binding, thus understood, reveals important features: it implies devious communications which mystify (Laing, 1961, 1965), interfere with the sharing of a common focus of attention (Wynne and Singer, 1963a and b), and disaffirm one's own or the other's messages (Haley, 1959). Such devious communications strain and unsettle the partner in the dialogue and they throw this dialogue off the track. Insofar as they unsettle the partner, they are *transitive* and *violent*. They violate his or her "cognitive integrity"; they wound him; they cause him to lose trust in his inner signposts, in his perceptions of himself and others, and in his most basic feelings. Such feelings—for example, feelings relating to our loving or being lovable—are always vulnerable to contrary attributions—i.e., to assertions that the person does not "really" feel this way or that he is only covering up, deceiving himself, etc. For these experiences cannot be confirmed by ordinary logic, by simple proof or disproof, or by recourse to an impartial arbitrator. To be validated, they must be subjectively asserted yet also be shared and exposed. But such sharing and exposure imply vulnerability to the violence of a cognitive binder.

L. Wynne (1972) has recently shown that such violence of cognitive binding can take two principal forms. It can occur either as an *injection of meaning* or a *withholding of meaning*. Where meaning is injected, the binder may label the bindee—for example, a spouse—as overworked and "nervous," while the latter sees herself as "merely" (yet justifiably) angry. The meanings "overworked" and "nervous" are here injected in order to substitute for the meaning "angry" as offered by the spouse. The latter is violated because the meanings "overworked" and "nervous" impute a self-image of weakness and helplessness while the meaning "anger" does not or does so less. This makes further understandable why attributions of weakness such as statements that the other is "sick," upset, sexually frustrated, or dependent generally have a stronger binding impact than attributes of badness—statements that the other is, for example, rebellious, cruel, mean, angry, etc. Attributions of weakness, much more than attributions of badness, impute as well as reinforce a continuing dependency on the supposedly stronger or healthier binder. Attributions of badness imply that the other person can eventually separate via rebellion and defiance, even though this may have to be achieved at the expense of a negative identity (Cf. Stierlin, et al., 1971).

Where binding operates mainly through the withholding of meaning, the binder remains essentially silent. Anyone who has treated families with silent members is likely to have experienced this binding stratagem. This member's silence increasingly unsettles all other participants. They seem anxiously glued to him and try to decipher his every grunt and blink while communication among themselves is paralyzed. When the silent member finally talks, frequently in brief and cryptic statements, his every word becomes the subject of the others' enduring, obsessive rumination and attention.

"Obedient" Self-Determination

The more dependent and immature the bindee, the more fateful the violence of the cognitive binder. The paradigm here is the parents' relationship to a dependent and immature child. We can speak of this child's cognitive thralldom to his stronger parent's reality (Stierlin, 1959).

The stronger binder can be violently coercive and yet can depict himself as well meaning and caring. Recently, M. Schatzman (1971) described how Daniel P. Schreber, whose paranoia was analyzed by Freud, was subject to such coercive binding by his father. The latter, a highly reputed educator and author, of whom even Freud spoke respectfully, acted as a sadist and persecutor while he trained his son to perceive him, the father, as loving and benevolent.

The same happened to countless victims of the Inquisition who were tortured by benevolent sadists who believed—and caused their victims to believe—that they acted out of concern for their victims' salvation. It also happened to those faithful victims of Stalin's purges, described by A. Koestler (1941) and others, who obediently accepted their stronger persecutors' definition of Marxist reality as well as of their (the victims') own motives and needs, including the need to let themselves be willingly executed. Such boundness of the victim reflects what we may call "obedient" self-determination, expressed succinctly by the heroine Iphigenie in Goethe's famous play of the same title, who states: *"Und folgsam fühlte sich meine Seele am schönsten frei"* ("Being obedient, my soul felt most blissfully free"). Here the cognitive binding seems complete. All awareness of having been bound, violated, and coerced has been abolished. Although he is wax in the binder's hands, the bindee believes himself to be free; and the coercive binder, the possessor of the stronger reality, instead of being (overtly) hated or feared, is venerated and loved.

Mutual Cognitive Thralldom

Although it makes sense to speak of a dependent and immature person's thralldom to the stronger person's reality, in practice such cognitive thralldom becomes mutual or transactional. This accords with our dialectical approach described earlier. There develops a circular, reinforcing yet highly restricting system of relationships, according to Wynne et al. (1958), wherein parents and children tend to act intermittently as binders and bindees to each other, thereby strengthening the binding bond. After a while, such a binding bond becomes nearly unseverable. Seriously cognitively bound couples and families therefore present the greatest challenge to therapy. For any intervention and any interpretation on the part of the therapist merely becomes material for further binding and leaves these patients as bound as before.

Where cognitive binding prevails, interpersonal conflicts, as commonly understood, are made difficult, if not impossible. For there is lacking that articulated separateness and distinctness of positions which is the sine qua non for the subjective experience of conflicts. Conflicts, instead, appear pushed underground and blotted out by a mutual retreat into what D. Reiss (1971) has called "consensus sensitivity." This is a seemingly conflictless yet regressive and muddy way of relating wherein it is more important to somehow atune oneself to the partner's emotional needs and wavelengths than to confront the partner via an individual and articulated separateness.

The Separation Drama of Cognitively Bound Adolescents

The stage is thus set for a particular type of drama. In this drama the adolescent's newly accruing reasoning skills, which were described earlier, become the critical element. These intellectual skills could become potent forces in liberating him from his parents. They could help him to critically compare his own feelings, motives, and goals with those of his parents. But, as matters stand, any such attempt to exert his ego assertively and discriminatingly is bound to raise the titer of his parents' anxiety, thereby redoubling their efforts to bind their child to them even more than before. Such an adolescent, hampered by an uneven development, yet more or less at ease with feeling cognitively bound (and with cognitively binding others), most likely will not be able to let his cognitive skills serve his drive toward autonomy. Rather, he will pervert his ideas into chains which bind him even more closely to his parents.

This happened to be the case with Max, a sixteen-year-old boy of superior intelligence. As he grew up, he became more inquisitive and started to read philosophical and psychological texts. His intellectual curiosity disturbed his mother. When he talked once at the breakfast table about ideas of C. G. Jung, she alluded to bookworm types who fail in life. Thus, she defined his intellectual and philosophical interests as weak, escapist cravings. Whenever she found him reading those "heavy books," she conveyed this message—more through her apprehensive, disapproving looks than through what she said. Occasionally, though, she lectured Max on the degenerate intellectuals in his father's family who either had killed themselves or had ended up in madhouses. She told him this, she said, only reluctantly out of her concern for his growth and well-being. When Max subsequently secluded himself to read or just to think, he noticed his pulse was hammering and his concentration waning. Was not this proof that reading and thinking were harmful, that they were evidence of his weakness and self-destructive streak, and that his mother (a somewhat high-strung woman, to be sure, but basically loving and concerned) was right? When he ventured timidly into the peer world, his apprehensions were confirmed. Being hypersensitive to being perceived as bookwormish, awkward, and inept, he acted awkwardly and ineptly and thereby invited confirmatory feedback. Increasingly, he avoided books as well as peers, and spent more and more solitary hours in his room, simultaneously watching TV and numbing himself with rock music. His room was adjacent to that of his mother, who did not mind the noise.

Again, this dynamic constellation is bound to affect and reveal whether and how an adolescent runs away. It explains why a number of disturbed adolescents could not run away at all or could run away only abortively. Having become accustomed to being bound, they were simply not up to the task of successfully relating with peers and other adults. When they tried to separate even temporarily, they were heading for a rude awakening because they could not deal effectively with the interpersonal peer reality that prevailed outside their family orbit. Like Max, they appeared deeply unsettled when they tried to move from the family culture into the peer culture. All seemed to badly lack skills needed for a life in a peer group or for dealing effectively with alternate adults. Many of them belonged to the group of "lonely schizoid runaways," described in Chapter 2.

For example, Emily, an attractive, relatively silent girl of sixteen, suddenly ran away from home, yet froze into a mute panic when a young man in the street asked her a question. A policeman eventually took Emily by the hand and led her home safely.

Emily had no friends at school and had never dated a boy. However, she could animatedly chat away with her family when no observer seemed present. All her cognitive skills seemed to serve her survival within an unusually binding and mystifying family field. When she tried to move outside, she experienced the equivalent of a "culture shock." She seemed totally at a loss when she had to deal with "normal," non-mystifying strangers.

Other adolescents seemed to "run away inwardly," to use a term of L. Wynne (1971). This indicates a deflection of cognitive growth into the build-up of a fantasy world which replaces the real world of living peers and alternate adults, and becomes *the* valued reality in these children's lives. This fantasy world, however, on closer inspection continues to interdigitate more or less with the fantasy world of other family members, despite its seeming idiosyncratic cast. I. Boszormenyi-Nagy (1965a), in particular, has described such interweaving of the family members' fantasies.

Abortive runaways of this type may run away in response to parental hassles. More frequently, they run off with little or no apparent overt parental provocation. While thus running away abortively, they appear mainly guided by their idiosyncratic introjects—offshoots of their fantasy world. Invariably, they strike us as very lonely runaways who nonetheless seem to be held on a long leash by their parents. In a precarious way, these children seem to try to make themselves at home in their fantasy world while they remain tied to their parents. They seem to unbind themselves in one sense while they remain bound in another. They appear both separated and unseparated, living in their own world and that of their parents, and yet not following the normal separation course of adolescence.

Binding Through the Exploitation of Loyalty

Certain parents contribute to yet another type of drama. This drama centers around the shift and modification of loyalties which the adolescent must achieve. At stake is the adolescent's successful final resolution of the Oedipus complex. Such a resolution would imply a successful, though relative, transfer of loyalty *away* from his parents and *toward* his friends, sexual and marital partners. This transfer of loyalty is dependent upon the adolescent modifying and/or attenuating his parental introjects so that he can cathect persons and values outside his family of origin in a relatively guilt-free manner. Parents can interfere with this process, however, by turning their children into lifelong, self-sacrificing, victim-adjuncts, a phenomenon which I. Boszormenyi-Nagy (1972) has described well. Adolescents who are chiefly bound on this level are likely to experience any thought of, not to mention attempt at, separation as the number-one crime for which only the harshest punishment will do. I am inclined to speak here of "superego-bound" adolescents. Attribution of weakness, as described earlier, is here an important element. But much more is involved. These parents convey—sometimes overtly, but more often covertly—that they have totally sacrificed themselves for their child, that they lived only *for him*. Also, they convey, through their actions and apprehensions, that they can live only *through him*, i.e., that they need him to supply their life's blood, as it were, that they cannot exist without him. Therefore, leaving his parents in either thought or action becomes the adolescent's worst crime. For leaving is now tantamount to the murder of his parents.

These adolescents are prone to suffer maximal primitive "breakaway guilt," a guilt that operates mainly unconsciously and gives rise to acts either of massive self-destruction or of heroic atonement. Primitive breakaway guilt, as intended here, intermeshes with, but also differs from, the type of guilt seen in many classically depressed patients who, while also bound and binding, try primarily to extract regressive gratifications.

Such archaic loyalty binding, too, colors any "separation conflicts" in adolescence. The threat of intense "breakaway guilt" operates here as a signal that warns the adolescent not to attempt to separate in either thought or action. Where he attempts such a separation, his "breakaway guilt" makes his conflicts unbearably intense. He can then resolve this conflict only by either destroying himself or ruefully returning to the parental orbit.

Such guilt-induced self-destruction appeared characteristic of certain of our abortive runaways of the lonely schizoid group. Roy, described as a lonely schizoid runaway in Chapter 2, is a case in point. I indicated that one night Roy began to drift around town in a lonely and bizarre manner. He was carrying a camera, which made him a desirable target for muggers. None bothered him that night, however. He finally entered the fifth-floor apartment of a strange woman, again a dangerous undertaking these days, with the result that he was arrested and then hospitalized in a psychiatric institution before the night ended. He is currently institutionalized in a psychiatric sanatorium with his mother living close by. She thinks almost constantly of Roy and tries to see him as much as she can, although she seems to court only rebuff and agony from him. Apart from Roy, there is little that could give meaning and direction to her life; she has few, if any, interests and friends, and feels suffocated in her marriage to an unloved, retiring husband whom she cannot consider divorcing.

In general, we expect the loyalty-bound adolescent not to run away at all. However, certain adolescents seem to suffer so much from intensified conflicts and ambivalences that, at one point or another, they run away regardless. When they do, they are, according to my observations, likely to fail spectacularly as their guilt will sabotage any chance of runaway success. We can therefore expect these adolescents to resume their conflicted and ambivalent ties with their parents at the end of their abortive runaway attempts—yet often under circumstances which further confirm them as victims *and* as failures. Rather typically, as the case of Roy demonstrates, they become hospitalized as psychiatric patients and as such remain the targets of their parents' unending, intrusive, though ambivalent, concern. Here again we find that the separation of the adolescent remains pathologic and incomplete.

THE MODE OF DELEGATING

This transactional mode is found in parents who react to their own developmental crisis with ongoing, unresolved ambivalence and conflict. Instead of settling on either a centripetal or centrifugal solution, as described earlier, these parents appear torn between centripetal and and centrifugal forces of seemingly equal strength. At one point they seek their salvation within the family; at another, they seem driven to flee the family orbit. They seem bent on consolidating existing relations and jobs, yet also seem compelled to make new starts. As their ambivalence intensifies, they turn to their children with conflicting expectations. They need to bind their children, but also to send them out. They want to benefit from them, but also need to be left alone and unhampered.

The term "delegate" denotes that the parents subject their children to these conflicting tendencies and hence to centrifugal as well as centripetal pressures. By making their child into a delegate they *send him out*, that is, encourage him to leave the family orbit. This meaning is conveyed by the Latin verb *"de-legare."* But also, while sending him out, they *hold on to him*. They entrust him with a mission, they make him into their proxy, their extended self. This second meaning, too, is contained in the original Latin word.

To the extent that parents succeed in recruiting their child as a delegate, it becomes his task to bear *their* ambivalence. He both takes it upon himself to cope with parental ambivalence, and makes himself into *their* reconciling agent. He fulfills this function often with ingenuity and skill, but always at the expense of his own genuine growth and separation.

If we turn to the dynamics of this delegating mode, we find that they include dynamics of the binding mode, yet with characteristic modifications and changes. Binding comes into play to the extent that the delegate, in addition to being sent out, must be induced to return home. The binding must be strong enough to counterbalance the "sending-out" component in the parent's behavior. But such binding, also, must operate more selectively and with a low profile, as it were. The parents must rely heavily on exploiting the delegate's unconscious loyalty, while they must relatively play down stratagems which bind the child on the affective and cognitive levels. For neither the affectively bound child who remains unduly captive to regressive parental gratification and hence lacks the motivation to move out, nor the strongly cognitively bound child whose distorted ego does not equip him to move into the peer group, has what it takes to become a "good" delegate.

The "good" delegate is not devastated by unconscious guilt should he move into the world of peers or alternate adults. He is not loyalty-bound in the sense that breaking away from the family becomes his number-one crime. His loyalty implies that he should become autonomous and skilled enough to carry out his special mission (or missions) and that he should experience guilt only when he fails, doubts, or rejects this mission. The phenomenology of his "loyalty boundness" differs therefore from the one found in more primitively loyalty-bound adolescents. We can speak of a selective and differentiated bond of loyalty that ties the delegate to his sender.

In addition to relating the dynamics of delegating to the dynamics of binding, we can consider them from another angle. Instead of focusing on how the parents' contributions bind the child, we can focus on the *mission* which the delegate must fulfill. This further clarifies those dynamic aspects which seem central to the delegating mode. In characterizing this mission we can, again, give transactional meaning to well-known psychoanalytic concepts.

The delegate's mission is dictated by his parents' needs. Typically, these needs would give rise to intensified internal conflict and ambivalence for the parent should he try to fulfill them without enlisting the service of the delegate.

The Conflicts of the Delegate

In taking it upon himself to carry out his parents' wishes and to resolve their problems and ambivalences, the delegate can become subject to two main types of conflict: *loyalty con-*

flicts and *mission conflicts*. These types of conflicts distort any other—more or less age-appropriate—conflicts he may experience over his individuation and separation.

Conflicts of loyalty arise when the delegate, in trying to remain loyal to one parent, is pitted against the other parent. Hamlet presents the paradigm of a loyalty conflict. He remained loyalty-bound to his dead father and was commissioned to destroy his mother. This embroiled him in deep and tragic conflict. The conflict of loyalties can also pit the adolescent's loyalty to the family as a whole against the loyalty he feels toward individual members.

Ordinarily, a child will align himself with the parent whom he perceives to be dominant, i.e., represents the stronger reality—similarly to the way a medieval vassal would try to align himself with the most powerful feudal lord. This explains why loyalty conflicts in a family are bound to become most fierce when the two parents are nearly equally dominant or when the balance of parental power shifts.

Conflicts between incompatible missions are also common. If the adolescent tries to execute them both, his conflicts deepen. Such conflicts of missions are aggravated by a conflict of loyalties. This occurs when a delegate feels beholden to both parents, who each expose him to their brand of incompatible missions. The different types of delegated conflicts become clearer when we consider, next, the various missions a delegate might have to fulfill. Table 2 may serve as reference.

The Delegate Who Serves the Parent's Elementary (Affective) Needs

It is the foremost mission of certain delegates to provide a parent with "id nutriment"—perceived to lie outside the family orbit—which the parent, for one reason or another, views as

TABLE 2

Major Missions of Delegates

A. MISSIONS SERVING THE PARENT'S ELEMENTARY (AFFECTIVE) NEEDS	B. MISSIONS SERVING THE PARENT'S EGO	C. MISSIONS SERVING THE PARENT'S SUPEREGO
Delegate must supply "id nutriment," i.e., must become a "thrill provider," thus often fulfilling a repair function for parents. Thrills may be shaped by exigencies of oral, anal, or phallic period.	1) *Simple helping or ego-support missions* Delegate must run errands, work in the house, etc. 2) *Fighting missions* Delegate must support embattled parent. 3) *"Scout missions"* Delegate serves as parent's experimenter 4) *Complex ego-support missions* Delegate must protect parent's fragile ego by sparing him heightened conflict and ambivalence.	1) Missions serving the parent's *ego ideal:* Delegate must fulfill parent's own unrealized aspirations. 2) Missions serving the parent's self-observation: Delegate must externalize (embody) the parent's disowned "badness." 3) Missions serving to alleviate the parent's conscience: Delegate must atone for the parent's disowned "badness."

unobtainable by his own efforts. Therefore, the delegate is sent out and expected to bring back to the parent the coveted nutriment which is then enjoyed by proxy. The parent experiences vicarious thrills, elicited by hints or vivid descriptions coming from the child, which stimulate the parent's imagination. These thrills, though avidly sought, can also conveniently be disowned by the parent. The child is scolded and punished for the very things he has been delegated to do.

The thrills can be primarily sexual. In this case, the parent covertly goads the delegate to engage in various sexual activities, including perversions and orgies, on which the parent wants to feed. Or these thrills may have a more oral, pregenital flavor. In this case the parent may covertly instigate and vicariously enjoy his child's drug or drinking parties. In other cases, these thrills chiefly have to do with wanting to do the forbidden and wanting to defy authorities. Such pleasures conceivably relate to vicissitudes of the anal period. In this case a parent covertly encourages and enjoys delinquent behavior in his child. But strong parental dependency needs of the clinging type, which play an important role in the binding mode discussed earlier, cannot be fulfilled by a delegate who is sent out and thereby allowed to loosen his ties to the parent. Therefore, if such parental dependency needs are strong, they will conflict with parental needs for having a thrill-providing delegate. In this case, the binding mode will most likely dominate over the delegating mode.

The delegate enlisted to provide vicarious satisfactions must often fulfill a repair function. He must provide his parents with experiences the latter missed when *they* were adolescents. He must now make up for his parents' aborted and frustrated adolescence; he must come up with a double dose of adolescent excitement, sufficient for his own and his parents' consumption.

The Delegate Who Serves the Parents' Ego

H. Hartmann (1950), building on Freud's basic discoveries, called the ego an "organ of adaptation and organization." In sticking to this broad definition, we can outline several types of missions for adolescents that strengthen or support their parents' egos.

All these missions imply that the child is allowed and

pushed to develop limited individuation, autonomy, and skills (or ego functions, if you wish), those required to carry out his missions. He is sent out and, held on a long leash of loyalty, he is also expected to come back.

A first type of ego mission can be called *simple helping or supporting*. A child or house slave is expected to help in the kitchen or in the field and, for this purpose, is allowed and trained to wash dishes, pick cotton, or run errands.

A second type of helping mission implies more complex dynamics. Here the parent seeks ego support and protection from the adolescent in his ongoing battles with other persons. These persons may be a hated spouse, an in-law, or an outside figure whom the parent perceives as persecuting and malevolent. It becomes the adolescent's mission to serve this parent as a faithful, unswerving ally in his battles, similar to the medieval bondsman who unwaveringly served his feudal lord. It is this mission for which Hamlet provides the paradigm, a mission most likely to embroil the delegate in loyalty conflicts.

This type of mission, like the others, ordinarily requires that the adolescent be sent out of the family orbit. If a mother enlists her son for the purpose of showing up her husband as a professional failure, she needs to encourage the son to move out and study hard so that he can become a professional success. Such recruitment of a son as a delegate ally may be prompted by the mother's ambivalent wish to break away from a marriage she finds distasteful and stifling. She exploits her son's sense of loyalty and uses him as part of a strategy designed to devalue and defeat her husband.

A third type of ego mission helps the partner to gather certain kinds of vital information. Such a parent may use the delegate as experimenter. This adolescent is expected to test out new solutions to his parents' conflicts or problems. These usually reflect the parent's ambivalent wish to break away from an existing job and family situation and to make a new start in life. In order for him to fulfill this type of mission, it becomes necessary that he be sent out (and be coerced to return). D. Reiss (1970) spoke here of the "scout function" of the adolescent. This adolescent is delegated to do something which the parent feels too afraid or to embarrassed to do himself. For example, a parent who wants to break out of the family and divorce his spouse, but is afraid of doing so, can use his adolescent for the purpose of obtaining firsthand information about what it is like to live by oneself. Also, a shy and retiring father who is afraid of dealing with authority figures can covertly delegate his son to battle with such figures. After having observed the son's more-or-less successful battling, he can conceivably dare to do it himself.

Finally, closely related to the mission of providing id nutriment and of serving the parent's self-observation (to be discussed in the following section) is the mission to support and complement the parent's defensive system. For example, a delegate who must provide his parent with id nutriment (e.g., must engage in orgies or smoke pot on his parent's behalf) may also have to alleviate his parent's anxiety, guilt, and conflict about needing such nutriment. His task becomes now more difficult as he, in addition to becoming profligate, embodying and enacting his parent's forbidden impulses, must also offer himself as a living screen for his parent's punitive projections. His major mission becomes, then, to maintain the parent's defensive organization, i.e., to "protect" and support his parent's fragile ego by sparing the latter heightened conflict and ambivalence.

This delegating mode comes into play when a parent enlists an adolescent son to resolve his own conflicts over delinquent tendencies. This parent covertly encourages his son to become a delinquent and then attacks him for doing so. He allows him to associate with delinquent peers and permits him to move out of the family orbit temporarily, yet awaits his return to mete out punishment. The delegate must be a delinquent and willingly submit to punishment as well.

The Delegate Who Serves the Parent's Superego

The mission here can pertain to any of the three functions which Freud (1933) attributed to the superego: to serve as ego ideal, to self-observe, or as conscience.

If the adolescent is delegated mainly to serve his parent's ego ideal, he will be sent out into life in order to fulfill those parental aspirations which the parent himself cannot realize. The adolescent is burdened with his parent's exaggerated and frustrated wishes to become an actor, scientist, physician, financial tycoon, etc.

If support of the parent's self-observation and self-confirmation becomes the adolescent's main mission, he will be delegated to provide a living contrast: to be bad. He is to be mischief maker, troubled, crazy, etc., in order for the parent to be reassured that he himself is not bad, crazy, etc., after all. This delegate must fulfill a function similar to that which the "inferior" Southern Negroes performed for their white masters when the latter found their own inwardly doubted superiority confirmed by constantly observing and confirming the Negro's "inferiority."

Finally, a delegate's main mission can be the alleviation of the parent's often excessively strict conscience. In this case, the adolescent will be covertly encouraged to commit and seek punishment for those delinquent acts about which the parent himself harbors (chiefly unconscious) guilt. Here the term *"superego lacunae,"* as suggested by A. Johnson and S. Szurek (1952), seems useful. The delegate is used to blot out these parental lacunae by making himself into the unwitting perpetrator of mischief and receiver of punishment. Here we typically find the adolescent who starts to steal in the same manner and at about the same time as did his father when the latter was an adolescent. The father can now comfortably tell himself that his own stealing as an adolescent could not have been so bad after all, as it is obviously an adolescent thing to do. Whatever residual guilt was left in the father will now be expiated by proxy, and he will continue to prompt his son to further punishment seeking.

This adolescent delegate becomes recruited to atone for his parent's assumed or actual wrongdoing. One can think here of certain German students who went to work in Israel in order to atone for their parents' crimes, crimes which these parents themselves could not consciously acknowledge. These youngsters called their action "sign of atonement" (*Aktion Sühnezeichen*). Their parents seemed to have succeeded in delegating—i.e., sending out to Israel—and unloading the pain of their guilt and repair work on to their adolescent children.

Delegates Who Run Away

I found that most runaways in our sample exemplified to varying extents certain of the dynamics of delegating outlined above. Particularly those runaways whom I have called "crisis runaways" reflect these dynamics.* As described in Chapter 2, they differed from the abortive runaways in that they were more successful in their runaway attempts. They managed to get away from their homes for rather extended periods and, at the same time, were able to become more persistently involved with their peers than were the abortive

---

* This characterization of the dynamics of runaways agrees only partly with that offered by R. Jenkins (1971), who was influential in including the "runaway reaction" in the *Diagnostic and Statistical Manual* of the American Psychiatric Association.

runaways. Yet these runaways seemed to differ also from the group of more casual runaways which, as we shall see, chiefly reflect the expelling mode. The "crisis runaways," under discussion here, typically seemed to run away in response to some manifest crisis within the family. Thus these youngsters, like the abortive runaways, appear subject to conflicting forces from their parents and from within themselves which affect the manner and style of their runaway ventures. These "crisis runaways" tend to relate more successfully to peers and therefore know where to run, namely, to some group or peer hangout, occasionally to distant relatives. Thus they manage to stay away longer than the abortive runaways.

Increasingly I came to see these "crisis runaways" as fulfilling various delegated missions, which often conflicted with each other yet nonetheless held the adolescent in their grip. Those runaways who chiefly served their parents' elementary and affective needs were delegated to bring back to their parents thrills and excitements which the parents could vicariously enjoy.

Lorraine, described in Chapter 2 as a crisis runaway, is here a case in point. The more Lorraine developed into an attractive, well-built, and slightly precocious teenager, the more her mother, grimly and excitedly, warned her of those wanton boys who were bent only on sexual mischief. This mother seemed obsessed with the possibility of Lorraine spending her nights with disreputable and orgy-prone young men. Not surprisingly, Lorraine confirmed her mother's apprehensions. She ran away repeatedly, as we saw, first to a nearby abandoned house, later to a distant metropolitan area where she, indeed, slept around with strange boys. This came to a halt after the family and Lorraine entered therapy (conjoint therapy for the whole family and individual therapy for Lorraine). Mainly through Lorraine's individual therapy it became apparent how much the girl had served as her mother's unwitting, thrill-providing delegate.

Bob, a boy of sixteen, provides an example of a delegate who acted out his father's unconscious delinquent wishes and tendencies. While away from home, Bob kept his father agonized and excited by one daring exploit after another. He engaged the police in reckless car chases, stole money by the most ingenious methods, outwitted pool sharks, etc. A. Johnson and S. Szurek (1952) have well described the manner in which parents instigate and recruit delegates for such delinquent missions.

Gary, also sixteen years old, demonstrated how an adolescent, in the very act of running away, can fulfill a parent's unconscious repair needs, that is, live out belatedly a part of this parent's own aborted adolescence. Gary, more than most other runaways in our sample, seemed motivated by wanderlust and roadside adventurism. After he returned home from a runaway episode of almost a month's duration, his parents—as well as his fellow patients and nurses on the ward—listened spellbound to the story of his exploits. He had gone to Mexico, had met many interesting people, had worked and slept at the most diverse places, making pale, so it seemed, the experiences of a Kerouac or "easy riders." Gary's father, I learned subsequently, had been deprived and pushed into a premature restrictive independence by his own parents and had never had a chance to satisfy *his* wanderlust. In the main, his adolescence had consisted of drudgery and study. He had dreamt of taking off, however, and visiting a certain area of the Mexican wilderness which for him was imbued with the romance of Indians and adventurous horsemen. It was this place that Gary, as if steered by a hidden, unerring gyroscope, had made the target of his runaway venture.

Tracy, another sixteen-year-old runaway, in response to her

father's covert messages, became self-destructively promiscuous and, in so doing, offered herself as a target for her father's punitive projections. In this way she took upon herself not only the mission of providing her father with exciting sexual id nutriment, but also that of keeping operational her father's ego defenses of denial and projection. Typically, Tracy would run away in response to some allusion or covert expectation of the father that she, Tracy, was a whore at heart. One evening, for example, the father read Tracy's diary, which he was not supposed to read but which was ingeniously placed in his way. It referred to her sexual interests in several boys. He immediately "confronted" Tracy with this evidence of evil proclivities. Tracy, then not quite thirteen years old, ran away later that night. Between the ages of thirteen and sixteen she ran away nine times. Each time she ran further away and stayed away for a longer period. Each time, also, she left some clue which made it possible for her father, by employing a detective's ingenuity, to trace her whereabouts—usually a hippy community in some metropolitan area—and eventually to rescue her. After the last rescue attempt, in which the father made use of police connections and underworld contacts, the family got into family therapy and Tracy received residential treatment. Family therapy revealed how much the father, a paranoid and potentially murderous man, had delegated Tracy to provide sexual excitement which he could also fight with sadistic righteousness.

Karen was another runaway in the crisis group. Her chief mission was to provide ego support to her embittered mother. This mother, who was the dominant parent, recruited the girl for the purpose of devastating her husband and thereby possibly breaking up a marriage that to the mother had become repulsive, stifling, and insupportable. Karen's mother hated, above everything else, what she considered her husband's restricted and restricting conventionality. In order to defeat him, she enlisted Karen as an ally. Karen ran away from home and—in the fulfillment of her mission—became sexually involved with a young black man who made his living from panhandling and pimping. The father, as was to be expected, perceived in his daughter's runaway escapade the ruin of everything he had worked for and believed in, while the mother praised Karen's daring unconventionality and inner freedom. As though to infuriate her husband even more, she invited Karen's lover into her home, where she treated him approvingly and flirtatiously. She continued to support her daughter's "honest experimental relationship" as long as it crushed her husband.

We turn now to the ways in which the runaways in our sample appeared to serve their parents' superegos. Here we have to deal, first, with the possibility of a delegate representing and fulfilling a parent's frustrated ego ideal. Dean and Donna, two runaway siblings aged fourteen and fifteen respectively, demonstrate how precipitous running away may become linked to the vicarious achievement of a certain type of parental ego ideal. Mr. Farmer, Dean's and Donna's father, had always lived in the shadow of his older, more successful brother, a banker and connoisseur of the arts. The brother had become a man of the world; adventurous, outgoing, and popular, he had done many interesting things and met interesting people. Mr. Farmer, in contrast, had turned into a restricted bureaucrat. Throughout most of his adult life, he spent his days adding up figures in a big office while enviously musing upon the adventurous careers and opportunities he had missed. In his first interview he spoke admiringly of Dean and Donna as being much like his older brother and different from himself. Whereas he saw himself as shy and timid, he saw Donna and Dean as daring, extroverted, and experimentative. As it turned out, they were experimentative with a vengeance. Whether it was experimenting with sex or drugs, with new life styles (such as living in communes), with being in the forefront of protest movements, Dean and Donna seemed to be always "where the action was." Not quite sixteen, Dean could boast of having become acquainted with more facets of life than his parents ever had or would. These experiences, many of them gained during his runaway episodes, included various delinquencies such as breaking into people's houses, pushing drugs, having sexual relations with black girls, associating with homosexuals, Black Panthers, taking part in gunfights, etc.

The self-observation and self-confirmation of the parents—the second superego function to be discussed—is served when adolescents, while running away, provide that living contrast of badness which the parents need so that they can view themselves as good and virtuous. This was the situation between Tracy and her father. Wherever runaway adolescents let themselves be enlisted as living screens for their parents' punitive projections, they serve this parental self-observing superego function.

Finally, I found in many of our crisis runaways the dynamics of parental guilt expiation by proxy. It seemed to me no accident that several of the runaway adolescents who tried to get away from home by means of a car (usually stolen) promptly created accidents. Other runaways seemed to have a knack for being quickly apprehended by the police (often on charges of possessing or handling drugs), when a minimum of circumspection could have avoided such fate. In contrast to the loyalty-bound adolescents described earlier, these "crisis adolescents" seemed to invite punishment not so much because they betrayed their primary loyalty to their parents, but because they, like Tracy, made it their mission to externalize, and invite punishment for, their parents' dis-owned "bad" impulses. One can therefore say that these run-away delegates remained loyal as targets for punishment by proxy.

THE MODE OF EXPELLING

In the expelling mode, again, the parents contribute to a dis-torted separation. And, as in the two earlier-described modes, they do so because they try to cope with their developmental crises.

The crucial element here is that the parents, in trying to solve *their* crises, come to view their adolescent children as hindrances. Whether these parents want to make new starts in life—for example, seek new partners, new jobs, new emo-tional investments—or simply want to find peace, their chil-dren, instead of being viewed as living assets that can be bound or delegated, appear burdensome and expendable. Therefore, these parents accelerate the centrifugal momen-tum inherent in the adolescent process, as they seem to have everything to gain and nothing to lose by pushing their chil-dren's early and definitive separation. These parents, in other words, expel their children because, in contrast to the bind-ing and delegating parents, they *do not want* these children.

Expelling can be viewed as a "sending out" minus the re-tracting, binding component inherent in the delegating mode. Expelling reflects an extreme centrifugal, and the binding mode an extreme centripetal, momentum whereas the dele-gating mode occupies an intermediate position, comprising centrifugal as well as centripetal elements.

When the expelling mode prevails, parents rebuff and

neglect their children. Either in a busy or in a withdrawn way, they seem so preoccupied with themselves and their own projects that they let their children run loose, as it were; they seem unconcerned when the children spend endless hours in front of the television set, experiment with drugs or precocious sex, skip classes, or roam around with delinquent gangs. In German, many of these children would be called *verwahrlost,* which has a somewhat different meaning than being merely deprived and neglected. These children are unduly left to themselves and constantly get the message: "You are expendable, the earlier you leave the home the better." Because the children are predominantly seen as nuisances, the emotional climate in these families differs from the one found in binding and delegating families. There is lacking the ongoing, though often conflicted and exploitative, investment in the child which gives the latter a sense of being important to his parents.

Runaways and the Expelling Mode

Adolescents who are exposed to an enduring expelling mode run away early and casually, without much ado. Realizing they are neither cared for nor wanted, they take to peer groups and alternate adults early and easily to the extent that their interpersonal skills equip them to do so.

It seemed unlikely that our sample of adolescents and families would yield many runaways who bore the imprint of the expelling mode, for I assumed that enduringly rejecting and neglecting parents are ordinarily not motivated to seek ongoing psychiatric help. There were, however, a few runaways in our sample who seemed to fit the above dynamics and typology rather well. These belonged to the group whom I have called "casual runaways." One of them was George, described in Chapter 2.

George was difficult to handle, and when his parents tried to control him, he threw tantrums and became obnoxious. For the sake of peace, his parents allowed him to "get away with murder." They just gave up control and, eventually, interest. George, bent on mischief, ran away from home, first for hours, then for half days, then for days. He ran away for several days at about the age of fourteen, after he had stolen some jewelry which he subsequently sold. His runnings away then became ever more casual and occasions for delinquent activities—usually carried out with buddies from his tough motorcycle gang. By then his parents no longer seemed to care. Eventually he was arrested for taking part in a burglary that netted several thousand dollars' worth of jewelry.

There were other cases in my sample who, though not as blatant as George, revealed neglectful and unconcerned parents. Rather typically, I needed to become enduringly acquainted—through psychotherapy and ongoing observation—with an adolescent and his family before I could appreciate the extent of the parents' insidious expelling and neglecting behavior. I have already mentioned the examples of Dean and Donna, whom their father enlisted as delegates in the service of his ego ideal and who became precocious separators and experimenters. In addition to using these children as delegates, the parents were neglectful and hence insidiously expelling. The father's presence as an executive, caring parent was almost nil, for he tended to gulp a few martinis before dinner and then, dreamily dozing, would withdraw from family life for the rest of the evening. He seemed unaware or unconcerned when Dean and Donna had sex and drug parties in their bedrooms or when they engaged in delinquencies. The mother, in spurts, tried to take the father's place as the family's limit-setter and organizer, but her parenting remained inadequate also. Much of her energies and time were taken up by unending hassles with her passive husband, whom she despised. She spent little time at home herself. Despite the fact that there were five children in the family—two of them below the age of ten—she had a full-time job which kept her away from home from eight in the morning until five in the evening. During this time, she left the care of the children to their schools, to makeshift arrangements, and to themselves. When she came home, she was tired, angered by her husband's alcoholic withdrawal, and quickly exhausted by the unsolvable task of checking on the children's accumulative delinquencies, absences, or passive-active avoidance of household duties.

As I have indicated, families with "casual" runaways seem more frequent in the larger population than my sample suggests. Presently it is estimated that approximately 40 to 60 percent of so-called street people, that is, permanent precariously adjusted runaways who live on welfare, handouts, short-time jobs, the sales of drugs, etc., have been rejected by parents who refuse to resume contact with them. Most of these runaways have probably been exposed to insidious neglect and rejection. The case of Mary Ann, although perhaps not quite typical, seems to illustrate the family dynamics which operate in the expelling mode here under discussion.

Mary Ann's story was reported by B. J. Phillips in *The Washington Post* of May 29, 1970. A follow-up story, written by Haynes Johnson, appeared in that same newspaper on March 21, 1971. Mary Ann, a fourteen-year-old runaway from a suburb north of Miami, became instantly famous when she was photographed crying beside the dead body of a student killed by National Guardsmen during the Kent State unrest earlier in 1970. Much of her parents' energies, instead of being channeled into the care of their children, seemed consumed by marital hassles. According to the policeman who handled Mary Ann's case in the juvenile court, her father "has been hot-tempered enough to go to jail for breach of the peace in Opalaka. The mother several times had sworn out peace warrants against her husband for disputes between themselves." Mary Ann's father worked as a carpenter and private contractor. He was quoted as saying, "I worked one hundred fifty hours a week for my family," indicating his unavailability as a father. All the other children in the family had become runaways with the exception of the youngest, who was three. A son, twenty at the time of the report, was serving a jail sentence for auto theft; another son, sixteen, the father of a four-month-old son, had been arrested for possession of marijuana. Mary Ann, while never having been charged with serious crimes, had begun to run away frequently and was regularly breaking the town's curfew from age thirteen. According to police, she had been on the fringe of adolescent drug use in Opalaka. Although the lengthy newspaper report gives many clues to parental neglect and rejection in the intended meaning here, the mother is quoted as saying, "Mary Ann wasn't neglected. She had the best clothes and all she could eat and she could go wherever she wanted to go. It was the school, not us." The very fact, though, that Mary Ann was always allowed to go where she wanted to go indicates to me that the parents lacked the kind of caring, limit-setting investment I have tried to emphasize.

Expulsions via enduring rebuff and neglect must be distinguished from those dramatic expulsions that chiefly reflect the dynamics of a binding or delegating mode. It is only in expulsions of the first type that we may speak of an expelling mode proper.

Dramatic expulsions of the second type may occur when the balance of modes in a family shifts. I indicated earlier that transactional modes may blend and that one mode may become more or less dominant over time. Dramatic expulsions, according to my observations, may signal a switch away from a binding or delegating mode. A binding or delegating parent, usually after agonizing inner turmoil and ambivalence, has decided here to get rid of his ill-begotten child for good.

Such a dramatic expulsion, while reflecting binding and delegating transactions which have reached a critical climax, may also reveal the additional long-standing operation of an expelling mode proper. Insidious, though covert, rejective parental tendencies may then come to the fore in such dramatic expulsion of adolescents who, till now, appeared mainly bound or delegated. Most frequently, however, dynamics such as the following seem involved.

The dramatic, climactic expulsion that follows prolonged binding or delegating parental efforts resembles the manner in which marital partners of long standing may try to separate. These partners, feeling trapped in suffocating ambivalence, can liberate themselves only by unleashing onto each other such an onslaught of rejecting hate and bitterness that they erase all chances for future reconciliation.

An expulsion which thus reverses a prevailing binding or delegating mode must be made to stick and hence must be backed up by some unmistakable and irreversible rejecting parental action. I observed such action, for example, when one father made up his mind to get rid of his twenty-year-old daughter whose seductive wiles he had so far ambivalently encouraged. In exasperation, he finally threw her down the stairs and forbade her to ever come back. He stuck to this decision despite the girl's pleading, wailing, and underhanded attempts to return home. Realizing that her father meant business, she eventually moved into another town where she made herself independent. This father, it may be added, could more easily adopt an uncompromising expelling stance because a younger daughter, no less attractive than the older one, was ready to fill her sister's vacated position. Another expelling father, after much ambivalent wavering, finally rallied his energies to get his son enlisted in the army. In so doing, he too tried to make sure that his expulsion would stick.

When an expelling mode proper prevails, the final expulsion seems by comparison undramatic. This expulsion appears, then, the logical sequence to ongoing parental rebuff and neglect, i.e., lack of concern and involvement. The child represents here for the parents some piece of cheap living furniture which can easily be used, abused, and finally discarded. When he seems useful he is, on the spur of the moment, cajoled, bribed, and manipulated; when he seems not useful, he is cursed, kicked, and pushed out of sight. Much anger and hate may be expended between these parents and their children, but neither do the anger and hate have the enslaving sadomasochistic, erotized quality we frequently find in the binding mode nor do they express deep disappointment and disillusionment due to the child's not living up to his parents' expectations or image. Instead, this anger and hatred are usually shallow and aroused by immediate, situational frustrations. Typically, such a parent beats his child because he left his bicycle standing in front of the parent's car, while he passes over unnoticed and unpunished the child's drug taking or disruptive behavior in school.

This difference between expulsions within, on the one hand, the binding and delegating mode and, on the other, the expelling mode proper, also affects the runaway picture.

Dramatically expelled adolescents, according to my observations, will often run away (either abortively or for longer periods of time) in ways which suggest they try to forestall, anticipate, or provoke the parents' expulsion of them. Larry and Gerald, two sixteen-year-old boys, serve as examples.

Gerald had a tortured, ambivalent relationship with his alcoholic father. This father badly wanted to spend time with Gerald in order to find solace for his alcoholic misery and loneliness. He pleaded with his son to stay with him, spoiled him with numerous gifts, and tried to bribe him. Gerald was tempted to give in to the father's binding stratagems but, at the same time, found himself wooed by his mother, thus suffering a conflict of loyalties. His mother viewed her husband as weak, contemptible, and a hindrance to her ambivalently coveted freedom. She succeeded in winning Gerald over as her ally and caused him to share her disparaging view of his father. The boy would ridicule, tease, and exasperate his father, thus nourishing the latter's resolve to get rid of the boy for good, painful as the operation might be. As time went on, the father's threats to expel Gerald became more ominous and the boy became more afraid, and hence more prone to run away. Gerald finally paved the way for his expulsion when he ran away for ten days. The father took this as a final proof of Gerald's incorrigibility and, by arranging for his hospitalization in another city, expelled him.

Larry, even more than Gerald, engaged his father in an intense sadomasochistic battle. Whatever father and son tried to do, they found themselves at once deadlocked in their bittersweet struggle. Larry, who was able to devise ever new ways of ridiculing and humiliating his father, ran away several times, each time in ways that enraged his father further. For example, Larry publicly smoked hash, thereby causing his father, a prominent figure in his community's antinarcotics program, to look ridiculous to his colleagues. Yet while away from home, Larry neglected his health so alarmingly that his father felt compelled to rescue him, and Larry, under protest, allowed himself to be rescued. Back at home, the sadomasochistic transaction resumed promptly until Larry, worn out and ambivalent, ran away again. This transactional pattern escalated over a period of two years to a point where the father finally evicted Larry, who then moved in with his mother—who was separated from her husband. After Larry broke off all contact with his father and settled down to live with his mother, he no longer ran away. Later, when he was approaching eighteen, he left his mother in order to enter a hippie commune. Both Gerald and Larry belong to the group of "crisis runaways." The crisis with which they had to cope was one of an intensifying ambivalence experienced by parent *and* child which engendered an expelling momentum. Once this crisis was resolved through their definitive expulsion, they no longer needed to run away.

In contrast, where a more insidiously rejecting parental attitude—i.e., a truly "expelling mode"—prevails, the runaway phenomena appear different as, I believe, the earlier examples of casual runaway show. In these examples, the children seem more to *drift* than to *run away*. If there is crisis and struggle in the family, these are relatively shallow and short-lived. What is overriding is the parent's enduring wish to get rid of his child.

5

Parents in Crisis and Separating Children: A Perspective on Disturbed Relations

---

In this chapter I shall illustrate in some detail how pressures for the binding, delegating, and expelling of children build up and how missions evolve. For this purpose, I shall focus on four families which have blends of modes. These families were seen as outpatients (in family, as well as couple, therapy), while their disturbed children resided on our adolescent ward and received individual therapy at least three times a week.

These four families represent a middle group that excludes the severe extremes of binding and expelling which will be the subject of following chapters. We excluded from our program extremely bound adolescents, particularly those with serious schizophrenic symptoms, *and* massively expelled ones. The first type of adolescents and their families appeared *unable*— i.e., too disorganized—to participate in our ward, work, and school program; the second type appeared unmotivated to do so. Expelling parents, uninterested and uninvested in their children, could hardly be expected to join a program that demands heavy sacrifices from them.

In describing these four families, I will selectively outline those salient dynamics which my above considerations and conceptual distinctions highlight. In an attempt to illuminate the disturbed adolescent's plight, I shall comment on the parents' life crisis, the state of their marriage, and each partner's relative dominance in the family.

MARIAN WALTERS: BOUND AND DELEGATED

The Parents

Mr. and Mrs. Walters, both in their mid-forties, had married in their early twenties. In marrying early, they had both tried to escape from squelching constriction and hardship at home—in vain, as it turned out. For their marriage, instead of liberating them, had brought them new chains and miseries. Twice Mr. Walters's small retail business failed and the family's finances remained in shambles most of the time. And compounding the financial problems were the demands made on them by eleven children born in rapid succession. Not surprisingly, the Walters looked exhausted and harassed when they applied for therapy. For years, they said, they had not found a quiet half hour during which they could talk about their intimate problems.

The spouses lived parallel to, but not with, each other. Their constant embroilment in pressing subsistence problems served to maintain a precarious marital truce. So did their fundamentalist Catholic faith which taught them to be forgiving and peaceable even under trying circumstances. Thus the parents had found an essentially centripetal solution to their marital and middle-age problems, a solution that precluded major new starts or liberating moves away from the family orbit. To understand further what such a centripetal solution implied for each parent, we can briefly consider the parents separately.

MRS. WALTERS

Mrs. Vivian Walters, the more dominant parent, presented herself as a strong, full-blossomed matron, who appeared neat, conscientious, serious, and controlling. Her stare, although intended to be kindly and warm, unsettled others and induced in them a vague sense of having done something wrong. Her strong and controlling exterior belied emotional impoverishment and restriction, however. As a child and adolescent, she had experienced little joy. Her parents, both stern and religious, had instilled in her a rigid puritan code and had successfully steered her away from boys who, in their opinion, could only lead her into sin and unhappiness.

Yet, by becoming a mother to many children, she hoped to fulfill belatedly at least part of her unsatisfied dependent and erotic needs. In one couple session, Mrs. Walters admitted that she gave birth to one baby after the other because her only enjoyment in life was having babies. By producing helpless, dependent infants, she could transform her passive dependent longings into an active, controlling counterdependence and, by caring for others, could come to grips with her own needs to be cared for. At the same time, in cuddling, bathing, and fondling her babies, she belatedly found some of the erotic gratification that her puritanical parents prevented her from finding through relating to boys or men of her own age.

Only young babies, however, could fulfill her previously unmet needs. Therefore, to remain happy, she had to go on producing new babies and dissociate the fact that babies grow up and create problems. The older her children became, the less such dissociation worked. For she was forced to realize that at least four of her children had been born with congenital defects and she had to endure disapproving and sniping remarks from neighbors. At one time, for example, she overheard a remark that she was an "overproducing womb." Such disapproval activated in her a core of doubts, shame, and guilt that in time gave rise to more or less veiled suicidal preoccupations. "The only reason I have not yet killed myself," she mused one day in the presence of her couple therapist, "is that I did not know which children to take along." True, she tried ever harder to be a good mother and she redoubled her efforts to keep her children well fed, dressed, and disciplined, but the guilt, shame, and doubts remained.

Her inevitable middle-age crisis hit her full force when, about fifteen months prior to the beginning of her therapy, she underwent a hysterectomy. This eliminated, once and for all, her chances of having more babies and of thereby satisfying her residual dependency needs. Feeling lonely, upset, mutilated, and guilt-ridden, she had to confront her horde of difficult and demanding adolescents and preadolescents while, at the same time, she had to fend off the explosive rage and frustration she felt toward her failing husband.

Clearly, in this family, Mrs. Walters was the dominant parent who, to all family members, embodied the stronger reality. In order to round out the picture, however, Mr. Walters also must be briefly mentioned.

MR. WALTERS

Mr. Walters's parents were less strict and Victorian in sexual matters than were his wife's. However, they so emphasized the value of early independence and achievement that Mr. Walters felt impelled to run away at age sixteen to prove to himself and his parents that he could "hack it." His two starts in business ended dismally, however, and he became demoralized. Such failure and demoralization subsequently shaped the image he and others held of him as a man, father, and provider. Whereas initially he had given promise that he could equal and counterbalance his wife's power in the family, he increasingly turned into a shadowy figure who proved no match for his wife. He no longer seemed able to protest when Mrs. Walters, the "executive" in the family, assigned to him household chores as if he were one of the children. This is not to imply that Mr. Walters was without major influence. In one sense, he was even more a target for his children's—and, in particular, his adolescent girls'—attention than Mrs. Walters, because he seemed more easygoing and openly flirtatious than his wife. But on closer inspection, this influence seemed in part delegated by Mrs. Walters. For although she was often manifestly irritated, frustrated, and jealous when Mr. Walters attracted the girls' erotic interest, covertly she tolerated or even encouraged these incestuous shenanigans. Being restricted, frigid, and fearful of a mature sexuality, she thus deflected her husband's sexual attention from herself and, in disapprovingly though excitedly watching the quasi-incestuous spectacle around her, she experienced vicariously some of the erotic thrills from which she felt excluded.

Let us, then, trace how some of the conflicts and problems of the parents' life crises—and, in particular, those of Mrs. Walters, the dominant parent—affected Marian, the fifth of the eleven children.

Marian Walters

Marian was fifteen and a half years old when she was admitted to our program. A medium-sized girl with a sallow complexion and sour looks, she appeared a living reproach to all around. Before we met her, she had been diagnosed as a depressed adolescent with psychosomatic troubles.

As indicated, Marian was the fifth of eleven children of which four had mild congenital (maternally transmitted and sex-linked) defects. Even though free of hereditary ailments herself, Marian, during the last year and a half before admission, had managed to monopolize the sickness scene among the siblings. This began two years before the time when her mother had her hysterectomy. At that point, Marian started to menstruate and changed dramatically. From an outgoing and seemingly normal girl who liked pranks and jokes, she turned into a sullen and sickly "problem child." She underwent a succession of diagnostic work-ups and hospitalizations for unspecified somatic complaints. She suffered intractable, though elusive, stomach pains, ate poorly, became emaciated and, after an exploratory laparotomy, was diagnosed as *anorexia nervosa*. Her frustrated physicians declared her troubles to be "psychiatric."

Despite this, Marian clung to her agonized, though "privileged," status as a somatic sufferer. Grimly trying to extract regressive gratification and nurturance from others, she was embattled with, and envied by, her whole family. Her underlying rage and guilt often seemed on the verge of erupting openly but, characteristically, tended to become channeled into suicidal threats and gestures, eliciting, in turn, guilt and rage in those living around her. Of all the children, Marian appeared most bound to her mother—in many respects, as we saw, the more powerful parent. She was closest to her mother and the most tuned into her mother's unconscious expectations, but also most fiercely embattled with her. (With her father she had a complex, incestuously charged, though less central relationship—here omitted—which also contained binding elements.)

CONFLICTS UNDER THE MODE OF BINDING

With her mother, the dominating parent, Marian appeared primarily bound-up on an elementary, dependency–needs level, as described earlier. She was less bound on the cognitive and archaic loyalty levels, as I have come to understand them, despite the fact that she engaged with her mother in a mutual sadomasochistic manipulation of guilt. With her fierce deployment of suffering and suicidal threats, Marian, like many classically depressed patients, gave evidence not so much of a primitive "breakaway guilt" that derives from an archaic loyalty boundness, but of a guilt that reflects as well as induces a sharp and refined struggle for dependent and regressive gratifications.

This distinction becomes even clearer when we consider those conflicts of Marian's which seemed chiefly determined by the delegating mode (once again, relating to her dominant mother). Four main delegated missions, each giving rise to specific conflicts, will be outlined.

CONFLICTS UNDER THE MODE OF DELEGATING

There was, first, the mission to serve as a selfless helper and supporter of the family. In this family of eleven children, of whom one or more tended to be sick at any given time, both parents had to work hard to make ends meet. Hence, they entrusted to the older children much of the care of the household and of the younger children. Such a helping mission, however, important as it seemed for the family's survival, conflicted with each child's wishes to have a life for him- or herself and to extract from others (chiefly the parents) regressive gratification and attention. Marian seemed most fiercely determined to extract such gratification and, for this reason, could not help defaulting most blatantly in her mission to be a willing and efficient mother's helper.

Second, Marian, like the other children, was entrusted with the mission to redeem and to prove unfounded the mother's inner doubts and guilt about having produced so many children, in spite of the fact that some of these had been born defective. This, we saw, was a major element in the mother's crisis of middle age. Stung by doubts and guilt, she was determined to bring up "good, well-behaved" children and she therefore entrusted her children with the mission of embodying her own virtuous ego ideal, thereby silencing the voice of her conscience. Of all her children, she found in Marian the most suitable and promising delegate for this second mission. But Marian seemed most conflicted about this mission: on the one hand, she seemed eager to embody her mother's virtuous ego ideal; on the other, she was unable to live up to her mother's expectations. She resolved the conflict posed through this mission by becoming neither *good* nor *bad*, but a *sick* child. Such "conflict resolution," in turn, was colored by the conflict arising from the third major mission which Marian's mother had delegated to her.

This third mission derived from that area of earlier-mentioned guilty concern in the mother which the latter, with only partial success, had tried to dissociate from her awareness—a guilty concern that was tied to her sense of having failed as a parent. I have mentioned how for a long time the mother had been preoccupied with the wish to kill herself. When looking at her children, we realize that she had tried to cope with her suicidal inclinations by recruiting the latter for the purpose of externalizing them. Unconsciously, she had delegated to these children the enactment of *her* suicidal tendencies in ways which allowed her to disown them and yet to keep them in sight as an issue for worried agitation. At least four of the children, we learned during our work with this family, at one time or another had made suicidal gestures or threats. Marian, however, seemed to externalize and embody the mother's suicidal tendencies most clearly. She developed sicknesses which seemed to presage a slow death and she flaunted suicidal gestures and threats which, at least in this hospital, focused the staff's attention on her. For weeks she appeared depressed and sullen, while she threateningly collected pills and sharp objects. This third mission, to externalize and enact her mother's suicidal inclinations, conflicted with other missions and genuine wishes to individuate and separate.

Finally, Marian was entrusted with a fourth main mission: to provide vicarious excitement. This mission, in order to be understood, must be seen against a background of mainly maternal attempts to foster—in the parents *and* in their children—a restrictive, almost Victorian, puritanical life style that was increasingly at odds with a surrounding society steeped in permissiveness and affluence. Marian, by being admitted to our adolescent ward, could not help becoming exposed to some features of the wider permissive and affluent society and youth culture. This, inevitably, stirred up temptations, ambivalences, and anxiety in Marian, in her parents, and particularly in her mother. Marian was here delegated to bear the brunt of her parents' ambivalences: she was covertly encouraged to provide some of the adolescent drug and sex excitement from which the parents and siblings cut themselves off. But also, she was recruited to serve as a living screen upon which the dangers and vices of permissiveness were cast into clear relief and hence could be safely and righteously fought. This fourth mission again subjected Marian to characteristic conflicts which made her individuation and separation difficult.

CONFLICTS UNDER THE MODE OF EXPELLING

Although Marian grew up in a large family where resources were limited, the parents harassed, and the fight for attention and recognition fierce, she did not strike us as a rejected or neglected child. I consider her as having been only minimally exposed to the expelling mode proper.

STAN MANNING: BOUND AND DELEGATED

Although bound and delegated like Marian Walters, Stan Manning had rather different conflicts over separation. Stan appeared more bound than delegated. Also, his boundness differed from that found in Marian. Whereas for Marian the binding mode operated mainly on the affective, dependency level, for Stan it operated more on the cognitive and archaic loyalty levels. Moreover, in his capacity as a delegate, he was exposed to different dilemmas and conflicts than beset the delegated Marian.

When Stan was admitted to our ward, he was considered a high risk for schizophrenia. Always a difficult child, he had become more disturbed and withdrawn around the age of fourteen. He fought with his parents, became obstreperous, lost interest in his schoolwork, and began to experiment with drugs. Increasingly, he looked lost and disorganized and spent a great deal of time daydreaming alone in his room. After an unsuccessful try at a psychiatric day-care clinic, full hospitalization became necessary.

He entered our program at age sixteen. He appeared arrogant, withdrawn, confused, and distrustful, while seemingly preoccupied with the functioning of his body and the dangers of cancer. His preoccupations had a delusional coloring.

Initially, it was doubtful whether he could stay on our open ward, where he appeared one of the sickest patients—i.e., potentially impulsive, rebellious, and "crazy." However, over time, he managed to participate in the scheduled activities (such as school, outings, patient self-government, etc.).

When considering Stan's conflicts over separation, we must keep in mind the fact that he, more than Marian Walters, was engaged with *both* parents, who contributed to the pertinent transactional modes more equally. Accordingly, we must specify how these modes referred to the father, the mother, or both. With this objective in mind, we turn now to Stan's parents.

The Marital Relationship of the Parents

At first sight, Mr. and Mrs. Manning's marital relationship resembled that of Mr. and Mrs. Walters. Like the Walters, the Mannings had found a centripetal solution to their marriage that precluded any thought of separation or divorce. And, like the Walters, they evinced a backlog of marital hatred, bitterness, and frustration that was precariously dissociated and controlled. But there were also differences. The Mannings were more closely bound up with each other than the Walters, exchanging—in pseudomutual fashion—more endearing words and sweet smiles than the latter. It is true, they bickered a lot in the privacy of their home and, in fact, could explode into rageful fits over a seeming triviality such as whether the air conditioner should be turned down or not. But somehow they managed to quickly dissociate or forget these outbursts and presented to outsiders a picture of sweet parental togetherness.

Such "sweet togetherness," in order to be operational and believable, required a special type of communication. While talking, each partner carefully avoided any clear-cut, and hence challengeable, position. Each partner thus steered away from clearly articulated disagreements. When disagreements loomed—for example, when Mr. Manning came out in favor of saving money and Mrs. Manning advocated the purchase of a new rug—they managed quickly to shift the focus and avoid confrontations. Mrs. Manning particularly seemed to contribute to a muddy communicational open-endedness by either anxiously babbling or remaining cryptic, silent, and enigmatic.

The Mannings, now in their mid-forties, had married more than twenty years ago. At that time, each partner promised to the other that which he or she most lacked, needed, and longed for. Mrs. Manning, sophisticated, vivacious, and labile, felt herself attracted to Mr. Manning's seriousness and reliability. Mr. Manning believed he found in his wife the spontaneous spark he missed in himself, the more so as this spark originated in a woman of charm and wealth. Instead of fulfilling its reciprocal promise, however, their marriage became centripetally stalemated. In order to understand this, we must briefly consider each parent.

MRS. MANNING

Although Clara Manning's background suggested wealth and prestige, she was not nearly as privileged as she looked, for her parents had separated when she was only six months old. She never saw her father, alleged to be an alcoholic. Her mother, beset by worries, handed Clara over to her own parents, that is, Clara's grandparents, with whom she lived until her early teens. Her grandparents, although meaning well and trying hard to accommodate this latecomer to their lives, afforded her little guidance and attention. Most of the time, she was left to the care of black nannies. In order to make up for their lack of attention, however, her grandparents spoiled Clara materially. While leading a life replete with parties and expensive glitter, she longed for loving—and limit-setting—parental stability. With the death of her grandfather in her mid-adolescence, the last vestige of such stability disappeared. Depressed and desolate, Clara returned to her mother, who by then had become a stranger to her. No wonder then she felt attracted to Mr. Manning, who impressed her as stable, reliable, kindly, and devoted. These (longed-for parental) qualities to her far outweighed his relatively low social background, which made him unacceptable to her extended family.

As was to be expected, Mr. Manning, the "father-husband," proved a bitter disappoinment and, as the marriage dragged on, she became more restless and desperate. She resented more and more that, for her husband's sake, she had alienated herself from her family and its wealth and, also, she resented and feared the decline of her beauty. A low point of her life was reached when she, like Mrs. Walters, had to undergo a hysterectomy that to her symbolized the loss of her femininity and grace.

MR. MANNING

Peter Manning, a haggard, depressed-looking man, felt alternately shame, anger, and pity for his parents who, as if to make up for lacking material goods and social amenities, fed constantly on a macabre diet of violent and perverse misdeeds committed, of course, by others. Nonetheless, they had tried to turn their two sons into models of propriety and forthrightness. They failed to achieve this goal with their older son—who turned "rebellious" and supplied further material for gossipy condemnations. Yet Stan Manning, by and large the more passive child, developed to their liking. He eschewed wild adventures and embarked on a restricted life of hard work and modest joys. To his parents, his only unpredictable and quasi-rebellious behavior occurred when he married his (in their opinion) exotic and outlandish wife. For this had the consequence of a gradually deepening estrangement from the parents themselves. He saw his parents less and less and, by the time he entered our therapy program, had lost almost all contact with them.

As if to atone for marrying a wife who was unacceptable to his parents, he soon gave up his promising college studies. Instead, he took on a tiresome and menial job as an assistant to a building contractor. This job required him to work long hours without real prospects for advancement. When he came to see us, he was worn out and had prematurely aged.

In our initial interviews we diagnosed Mr. Manning as a compulsive and depressed personality. Later, we also noticed a stubborn paranoid streak, particularly directed toward his female cotherapist. Toward his male therapist, who happened to be also his son's therapist, he related in a persistently obsequious and idealizing manner that had homosexual undertones.

Two children—Katherine, age nineteen, and Stan, age sixteen, at the time of admission—were born to the Mannings. And, as could be expected, both of them became recruited to alleviate and possibly resolve their parents' plights and middle-age crises. I shall, in the following, limit myself to sketching out what this implied for Stan.

CONFLICTS UNDER THE BINDING MODE

Cognitive binding through the mother. In the family sessions, no less than in the couple sessions, the mother tended either to anxiously babble or to remain cryptic, silent, or enigmatic. Her silence and cryptic utterances came to the fore mainly in later phases of family therapy, proving to be powerfully binding on the cognitive level.

In therapy, this process was manifest as she just sat there, an enigmatic smile on her face, and let the other family members fumble along in their efforts to make sense of what she (the mother) did or, more correctly, did *not* communicate. By excluding herself as a validating agent, she presented the other family members with the alternatives of either ignoring and excluding her as a contributing member, or of having to adopt a less articulate, more emotional, more primary process mode of communication into which her enigmaticness could, hopefully, be absorbed. In this mode of communication, a consensus sensitivity, in the terms of D. Reiss (1971), became operative. The family shunted uneasily back and forth between the two communicational courses, either ignoring the mother or adopting her imposed consensus–sensitive mode. Neither course, though, allowed Stan to differentiate himself from his mother in an articulated and confronting manner. Stan—and with him the other family members—remained mystified, unsettled, and yet tied to his mother; that is, he remained cognitively bound to her.

Being thus subjected to "cognitive binding," it seemed no wonder that Stan was able to remain differentiated only precariously in interpersonal situations requiring empathy or closeness. In such situations, he was threatened by a loss of boundaries and hence was driven either to adopt a rigidly arrogant, "paranoid," distancing stance, or to withdraw into a world of fantasies and drugged numbness. Both reactions indicated that Stan lacked the will and/or ability to relate deeply to peers and alternate adults.

Stan bound by archaic loyalty. Various aspects of Stan's appearance and behavior caused me to infer that he, bound by archaic loyalty, felt threatened by "breakaway guilt." Such guilt can devastate an adolescent who has learned to experience any attempt to separate, in thought or action, as the number-one crime. Compared with other potentially schizophrenic adolescents, however, his archaic loyalty boundness appeared moderate.

There was, first, Stan's appearance. He impressed observers as a "martyred Jesus," destined to save, and to suffer for, others (i.e., his parents). He visibly demonstrated a phenomenon which I have observed in other archaically loyalty-bound adolescents—the compulsion to become the family therapist and rescuer. Such a compulsion, I believe, serves in part to counteract intense breakaway anxiety and reflects the need to atone for "breakaway guilt." This is congruent with the posture of the willing victim, which I. Boszormenyi-Nagy (1972) has detailed well, a role which seemed inscribed on Stan's angelic, martyred face. But further, in order to atone for "breakaway guilt," Stan needed to ensure that he, in attempting self-assertion and separation, appeared inept and/or wicked. For example, he managed to be "busted" quickly by the police when he made a tentative, short-lived runaway attempt typical of the self-destructive, "abortive runaways," described earlier.

Through binding Stan on the cognitive and archaic loyalty levels, Mrs. Manning ensured that Stan, at the time of her deepening despair and crisis, would remain tied to her, for good or for bad. For the bound Stan, this implied that his conflicts over separation remained suspended. At the same time, they remained threateningly explosive. Some of the explosiveness surfaced when Stan, approximately six months after his and the family's uneasy and complicated withdrawal from our program, had to be treated elsewhere as an emergency. In an apparent suicidal attempt, Stan had then swallowed a variety of unspecified pills.

CONFLICTS UNDER THE DELEGATING MODE

Stan as delegate. Stan, like Marian, was bound *and* delegated. However, while Marian, as a delegate, chiefly experienced a *conflict of missions*, Stan primarily experienced a *conflict of loyalties*. Stan, we saw, was nearly equally, though differently, embroiled with both parents, whereas Marian had been embroiled mainly with her mother. (Stan, also, evinced a conflict of missions but, for the purposes of this exposition, I shall focus on his conflict of loyalties.)

Stan entrusted with mother's mission to destroy father. We noted that, as a marital couple, Mr. and Mrs. Manning, although exuding endearing sweetness, were embattled in frustration and rage. Therefore, unable to conceive of separation, they could not help recruiting their children as personal allies. The father found his ally in Katherine, Stan's older sister, to whom he related intensely and quasi-incestuously. The mother, perhaps by default, chose Stan. Stan's involvement with mother then provided the base for her entrusting him with the mission to destroy his father.

Stan's mission to destroy his father became apparent as the family therapy progressed. While retreating into enigmatic silence, the mother would, gleefully and amusedly, watch Stan denounce his father as stupid, brutal, and obsoletely authoritarian. When the two men sought reconciliation, she would —more or less covertly—egg Stan on to berate his father further. In a half-questioning way, for example, she would hint at father's weakness or failure as a provider, thereby, in renewed oedipal promise, boosting Stan's flagging fighting spirit.

Yet Stan, while loyally trying to fulfill his mother's mission, tried also to fulfill missions entrusted to him by his father. Hence, a conflict of loyalties was unavoidable. The father appeared to entrust Stan with two missions: first, to embody and enact father's dissociated badness and, second, to provide father with fatherly warmth and understanding.

The first mission can serve a parent's self-observation. The adolescent delegate, as we saw, must provide the living contrast of badness (or craziness) which the parent needs in order to remain reassured about his (or her) own virtue or sanity. Such a delegate, we found, fulfills a similar function as a slave did for his master who needed the slave's "inferiority" as a constant reminder and reassurance of his own "superiority."

Mr. Manning had been the "good" boy who, throughout his adult life, held a tiring, routine job that offered no chance for advancement. Restricted, compulsive, and depressed, he had to fight in himself intense wishes to "goof off," to break out of the rat race, and to "screw the establishment." Also, he envied his older brother who, as mentioned above, had "succeeded" in becoming his parents' delegate for the vicarious experience of mischief. Stan offered Mr. Manning a belated chance for drawing even with this envied brother. Stan now embodied and enacted Mr. Manning's disowned wishes by skipping school, by drifting into the hippie and drug world, and by defying the values of the establishment. And Stan enacted these wishes in ways which permitted Mr. Manning not only to disown them, but also to attack them punitively and righteously, just as his parents had attacked such disowned wishes in his brother.

In addition to serving his father as a living screen for his disowned, punitive projections, Stan also, through his infighting, gratified some of his father's needs for closeness and involvement. Through fighting his son, Mr. Manning could relate to the latter in a manner that promised to fulfill intense needs for nurturance and self-confirmation. These needs, too, had remained unsatisfied in his relations with his own parents (and particularly with his father) and currently with his wife. In brief, through fighting Stan, he could hope to *parentify* his son. These fights, it is true, implied distance between the fighting partners yet also, as time went on, could turn more and more into "loving fights," to be elaborated in a later chapter, that enhanced the fighter's respect and understanding for each other.

But any move in the direction of a "loving fight," and hence of an eventual reconciliation with the father, was bound to conflict with the mission which the mother had entrusted to Stan—the mission to destroy his father. Therefore, Stan could not escape a conflict of loyalties.

CONFLICTS UNDER THE EXPELLING MODE

Although Stan, at times, seemed to disengage himself dramatically from his parents, this did not happen under an expelling mode. Instead, Stan appeared to disengage himself by trying to find a niche and retreating into a fantasy world, as seems typical for adolescents in certain strongly bound-up families.

JASON TENELLI: BOUND AND DELEGATED

Jason, like Marian and Stan, was bound and delegated, yet reflected still further variations in separation conflicts.

Jason, the fourth of five boys, had just turned fifteen when he was admitted to our ward. He had been labeled, legally, an uncontrollable delinquent because about a year and a half earlier he began to be truant from school, to forge report cards, to steal money from his parents, and to stay out all night. He spent these nights with older boys, and his parents felt he took drugs and associated with homosexuals. He was repeatedly institutionalized. A crisis arose when he refused to enter a detested detention home. At this point, he swallowed approximately a hundred cough tablets and, in a blackmailing ploy, was hospitalized as a medical and psychiatric emergency. A few months later he was transferred to our program.

The Marital Relationship of the Tenellis

Like the Mannings and the Walters, the Tenellis were in their mid-forties. Financially they were well off due to Mr. Tenelli's success as a civil engineer. Their social backgrounds —both came from lower middle-class parents—were more compatible than those of the two other couples.

Mr. and Mrs. Tenelli tried to project an image of essential marital harmony. From the outset, they said, their marriage had been fine and smooth. There were no financial problems, no marital problems; there were problems only with the children. Thus, these parents lacked any awareness of a middle-age crisis. They had worked out a centripetal solution to the tasks of marital life that, to them, presented no cause for distress.

As the family and couple therapy unfolded, however, this picture changed. Problems came into sight that were hardly less severe than those of the Walters and Mannings. In a sense, it was the spouses' assertions that nothing was wrong with them which constituted the biggest problem. For such assertions amounted to a denial that blocked any chances for changing things between them—except through the services of their children. No wonder that in their relationship to these children, but particularly toward Jason, they showed as much upset, frustration, and helpless rage as they showed harmony in their relation to each other.

MR. ALFONSE TENELLI

Mr. Tenelli, of Southern European descent, was lively and effusive. When he was present in family sessions, everybody was animated and alert; when he was absent, depressive lethargy and silence crept in. No one could doubt he was the dominant parent.

But, although warm and effusive, Mr. Tenelli was not introspective. He had a mechanic's mind that turned any problem—be it technical, moral, or esthetic—into one that could be labeled good or bad and be handled by practical formulas. In applying his engineering approach to human problems, Mr. Tenelli was unempathic. Psychological complexities eluded him. Yet, in a vague way, he seemed intrigued by, and attracted to, persons who could operate on finer emotional wavelengths than his. As Mr. Tenelli's therapist, I often asked myself what might underlie his lack of empathy and psychological-mindedness. His early upbringing and family background gave only uncertain clues. Again and again, he emphasized that his father, a poor European immigrant, had instilled in him the value of hard work while shielding him from the bad boys (and girls) who were roaming their poor slum neighborhood. While his peers roamed, he studied and eventually managed to win academic honors and business success.

Only in the course of his present therapy did he begin to reveal a gnawing, though inarticulate, suspicion that his life might remain unfulfilled. He had, in fact, experienced little of a "real" adolescence and, as it turned out, had not acquired the tools and interests needed to make his middle years rich and varied. Apart from his work, which had become routine, there were the football games and occasional outings on weekends and there were, above all, his children—yet now all preparing to leave.

MRS. TERESA TENELLI

As a spouse, Mrs. Tenelli seemed much less engaging than her husband. Observers found her cold and empty despite her pretty face and attractive exterior. On the whole, she was less able to provide her children with maternal nurturance than Mr. Tenelli. Closer inspection revealed that her actual life, despite (or because of) its suburban shelteredness, was as empty as the expression on her face. There was little for her besides chauffeuring the children, going to a weekly bridge club, making candles, and watching soap operas on television. Nonetheless, as therapy progressed, she showed some sparks. In a mood of hysterical giddiness, she could tell and laugh about dirty jokes and also, in a mixture of triumph and contempt, could decry her husband as compulsive and immature —just as her children were. Gradually she revealed more of her underlying depression, her sense of deprivation and unhappiness, and her resentment of her husband's excessive involvement with the children.

Let us, then, consider how Jason was recruited to resolve some of the problems which Mr. and Mrs. Tenelli could neither recognize nor resolve in relating to each other.

CONFLICTS UNDER THE BINDING MODE

Jason, like Marian, was chiefly embroiled with *one* dominant parent, his father. The father was his main binder and delegator. An authoritarian and vocal man, he appeared anxious, accusatory, and helpless in dealing with Jason, thereby testifying how much his life centered around the boy. Mrs. Tenelli, the colder and more reserved parent, kept herself in the background, yet occasionally stepped into the discussion, often in order to attack her husband and sons in veiled ways.

The more we saw of Mr. Tenelli, the more we found him wooing Jason in the fashion of a frustrated lover. On a deeper level, we found Mr. Tenelli binding his son in an attempt to receive from him the warmth and nurturance he himself had missed as a child. He showered the boy with gifts, attention, and promises. Thereby he also made sure that he had a tiger on his hands once Jason, spurred by his intensifying libidinal and aggressive drives, came to feel more ambivalent about his father's "courtship" of him. Indeed, when he entered our program, Jason was overwhelmed by the threat of a squelching closeness with his father and, in particular, was threatened by its "homosexual" undertones. No wonder that on admission he was near panic, and torn between wishes to escape and to stay. But his panic notwithstanding, he had, to outward appearances, turned into a tiger. His power to induce, by a snap of his fingers, happiness, despair, or impotence in his father intoxicated and bewildered him.

Jason was bound not only on the elementary dependency level but on the cognitive level as well. The phenomenology of such cognitive boundness, however, differed somewhat from the one found in the case of Stan. Jason's father, singularly unable to empathize, could not tune himself perceptively to his son's emotional wavelength. He seemed also singularly unaware of many of his own needs, motives, and feelings since emotional problems for him tended to become simplistic "good–bad" problems, problems that could be properly engineered.

To the extent that the father managed to disown his own conflicts and needfulness, Jason had to serve as his "problem provider." And Jason obliged. Dutifully, he provided problems that were sufficiently concrete to suit his father's unempathic engineering and "law and order" approach. He stole, took drugs, forged report cards, stayed out late at night, etc. Thus he confirmed his father's definition of what the problem was and adapted himself to his father's "stronger reality." In this process he substituted his father's distorting for his own discriminating ego, as we found typical for cognitive boundness.

The family therapy sessions provided insights into how

Jason was coerced into becoming the father's problem provider. For example, even when Jason behaved well on the ward and on the outside, his father would approach him anxiously and accusatorily, stating, "We have no reason to believe you have improved; let us know what happened yesterday on the ward." Inevitably Jason, at least early in family therapy, would get into angry, argumentative hassles and in defiant provocativeness would eventually admit some misdeeds, or at least a disposition to misdeeds, thereby adjusting to his father's "stronger reality." Such cognitive boundness, when combining with certain forms of delegating, can induce delinquency quite powerfully in adolescents, as we shall see shortly.

Finally, Jason was bound also on the archaic-loyalty level, though less severely than I have observed to be the case in some families. The father exhorted his children always to subordinate their needs to those of the family, as he advocated strong family ties, which were part of his own cultural heritage. Along with instilling in his children a strong family loyalty, he also laid the ground for "breakaway guilt." Yet such loyalty and "breakaway guilt" pertained not so much to the family as to the father alone. For it was he, ultimately, who defined the meaning and boundary of the family. Typically, he talked in terms of "we" (the family) when he, in fact, meant "I"—his own wishes, needs, and boundaries.

Bound by an archaic loyalty, Jason's attempts to break away or run away from home remained understandably abortive. Therefore Jason serves as another example of abortive runaways who, in the very abortiveness of their runaway attempts, testify to the strength of the bond that ties them to their parents. Also, in Jason's case, the self-destructive and punishment-seeking features in his abortive runaway behavior gave evidence of how, unconsciously, he experienced his breakaway attempts as crimes that deserved harsh punishment.

Yet Jason's conflicts under the binding mode do not sufficiently account for all important aspects of his pathology and particularly his delinquent behavior. In order to understand these aspects, we must turn to his separation conflicts developing primarily under the delegating mode.

CONFLICTS UNDER THE DELEGATING MODE

As his father's delegate, Jason was expected to fulfill two major missions: to become an academic superachiever and to provide excitement. Both missions grew out of the father's unresolved life problems as sketched above. And both missions implied that Jason was to be sent out of the family, but that he was also to be held on a long leash. Neither mission, however, meshed with the kind of close-knit family which the father otherwise tried to foster. Moreover, the two missions— to become a superachiever and an excitement provider—were inherently incompatible with each other and thus represented another example of a "conflict of missions."

From the beginning, Jason's first mission—to become an academic superachiever—was headed for failure. His temperament and intellectual make-up, since he was neither studious nor brilliant, made it unlikely that he could live up to the father's enduring expectation that he become a shining academic light. This was the more unlikely, as the role of the family's superachiever had already been filled by his older brother, Richard. Richard seemed headed for academic honors, and Jason seemed to content himself with the "negative honor" of being a troublemaker and underachiever. This, according to my observations, is one way an adolescent can try to cope with such a "mission impossible."

Failing in his first major mission, Jason seemed determined to succeed in his second mission to become an excitement provider. This mission, typically, owed its importance to the father's own adolescent experiences—or better, lack of experiences—and repair needs. Mr. Tenelli had foregone many adolescent enjoyments because his father had driven him to work hard so that he, and his father, could rise socially. Now Mr. Tenelli delegated to Jason the mission to make up for some of his own lost youth. He now expected to experience through Jason adolescent excitement by proxy, as it were. For this purpose, he triggered and encouraged his son's delinquent behavior. The suburban dullness and restrictiveness of his parents' lives contrasted sharply with the excitement provided by Jason's wicked adventurism. In recruiting Jason as an excitement provider, the father joined forces with the mother who, in her "hysterical" giddiness, was disarmingly revealing. When the couple's therapist tried to explore the background of Jason's delinquencies, the mother explained, "Oh, I think things were just too dull at home." The parents, we learned later, had deliberately put minor sums of money into Jason's path in order to test whether he would or would not steal. As could be expected, Jason "failed" this test.

But Jason, in addition to serving as an excitement provider, was to serve as a problem provider. It was, I believe, this combination of parental expectations that primarily produced Jason's brand of delinquency—a delinquency characterized by an anxious boundness to his father, combined with self-destructive punishment seeking and abortive runaway attempts.

CONFLICTS UNDER THE EXPELLING MODE

Jason seemed only minimally exposed to an expelling mode proper, notwithstanding the fact that his father, at times, appeared to reach a point where he seemed ready to expel Jason for good. Precipitous, dramatic expulsions which may or may not last are, we saw, typical of family relations such as those of the Tenellis, wherein a strong binding or delegating mode dominates.

GAIL DIXON: DELEGATED AND EXPELLED

Gail, like Jason, had been labeled an uncontrollable delinquent prior to entering our program at age sixteen. Like Jason, she was truant and unruly, and had been confined to detention homes. Yet unlike Jason, whom I have classified an abortive runaway, Gail had run away on a large scale. Also, there was a longer history to her troubles than Jason's. Often appearing cynical, Gail was more skilled and hardened in exploiting and manipulating people than Jason. At the same time, she impressed me as a deprived and affection-starved girl who suffered from a "neurosis of abandonment," as described by C. Odier (1956). She was constantly driven by a need to cling to any person who promised her some human warmth; yet she seemed, at the same time, unable to tolerate relational ambivalence and complexity, with the result that she quickly needed to get away from "boyfriends," therapists, or therapeutic settings such as hospitals and detention homes. Not surprisingly (after only a few months), she ran away from our program also.

Gail's brand of delinquency (i.e., her "casual" running away, affection starvation, and a tendency to manipulate and exploit others) becomes more understandable when it is analyzed under the three modes of binding, delegating, and expelling. In order to do so, we must, again, briefly look at the parents.

The Marital Relation of Mr. and Mrs. Dixon

In contrast to the three families described earlier, the Dixons were in the grip of strong centrifugal forces. Two years earlier they had decided to live separately in different apartments. Even earlier they had pursued different interests and both had had extramarital dates and affairs. Still, they had avoided a complete rupture of their relationship. They continued to get together rather frequently—ostensibly to discuss the children, who lived with Mrs. Dixon—and occasionally even had sexual relations with each other. From the beginning of the couple and family therapy, they expressed mutual disappointment and berated each other bitterly.

Mrs. Dixon pointed, above all, to her husband's irresponsibility and drinking. He had squandered a large inheritance of hers and subsequently had been fired from one job after another.

Mr. Dixon, in turn, emphasized how his wife, instead of building him up, had depreciated and demoralized him.

Closer inquiry revealed that both spouses had been married before—Mr. Dixon twice. In these earlier marriages there also had been much angry fighting, infidelity, and, at times, abortive attempts to separate. But then, as in the present marriage, they seemed to have found it difficult to make the final break.

By the time we saw the Dixons, Mrs. Dixon had emerged as the dominant parent. She was more energetic, more driven, more powerful than her husband, who presented himself as obsequious, helpless, and downtrodden. As it turned out, though, Mr. Dixon also had some power left in him.

MRS. JEANNE DIXON

Mrs. Dixon grew up in a home that resembled the one she was offering her children—a home with two fighting parents who used to go their own ways and who constantly threatened separation (which, however, never materialized). As both of

Mrs. Dixon's parents espoused "culture," they gave their home a Bohemian touch. Her mother dabbled in singing and painting and conceived of herself as an artist, whereas her father, the more peaceful and passive partner and parent, projected the image of an art connoisseur.

As an adult, Mrs. Dixon became much like her "arty," erratic, and intrusive mother. Like her, she was always on the go, fired by some "creative" project that promised artistic fulfillment and financial success. But she lacked the stamina, talent, and education needed to realize her dreams. After each failure, she would embark on a new project and, more intensely than before, would look for the man who, by his strength, patience, and devotion, would sustain her drive, yet cure her of her "drivenness."

After her first marriage ended, Mrs. Dixon believed she had found this kind of man in the person of Mr. Dixon. At first sight, Mr. Dixon inspired her confidence because he appeared dignified and responsible. But, as time went by, she was forced to reverse her opinion. Not only did Mr. Dixon's dignified, quiet exterior hide a timid passivity; he also proved to be irresponsible and, at times, delinquent. He squandered her inherited money on whiskey and stock operations, and lied and cheated.

Mrs. Dixon's troubles mounted when, five years prior to her seeing us, she was found to have cancer of the breast. Although a mastectomy seemed successful, Mrs. Dixon became ever more frantic in her need for new starts which, this time, seemed to have brought success within her reach. Shortly before seeing us, she was offered a chance to open an art gallery and also met a new boyfriend (a man influential in the art business). But while new opportunities beckoned, she also, in deepening ambivalence, had more qualms about leaving her husband. Therefore, she agreed to participate in couple and family therapy even though she considered her marriage on the rocks.

MR. KARL DIXON

Karl Dixon seemed no less eager than his wife to join the therapies—"for the marriage and the children's sake"—and, in so doing, conveyed motivation, reasonableness, and responsibility. It was hard to believe that his wife should see him as an irresponsible and delinquent drunkard. The facts which emerged in individual and couple therapy sessions, however, lent at least some credence to his wife's accusations.

Mr. Dixon came from a family of twelve children. He learned to despise his mother who, cold and unapproachable, spent her afternoons and evenings playing bridge while her twelve children were left to the care of their father, grandparents, and each other. Lacking consistent parental guidance, he learned early to play hooky. He missed school often and, in high school, he stole minor sums of money, cheated, and lied. After leaving school, however, he slowly seemed to find himself. Perhaps helped by his dignified, responsible exterior, he had success as a salesman. His drinking, which had troubled him and others from time to time, came under control. But gradually marital stresses intensified and resulted in the breakup of two marriages. Luck and hope seemed to take hold of him again when, in his mid-thirties, he married Mrs. Dixon, who was then beautiful, artistic, and wealthy.

At the time we saw him—in his mid-fifties, approximately twenty years after the start of his third marriage—he, like his wife, had not given up the hope of making a new start despite his many disappointments. Although he had been fired recently from his job, he was again looking into new possibilities and also contemplated a new marriage, his fourth.

Let us now consider how all this bore on Gail, the Dixons' oldest child, who became our patient.

Gail's Situation

Neither of Gail's parents was dominant in the previously developed sense of the term, as neither seemed really intensely invested in her. Because of such reduced investment, the kind of sustained interpersonal conflict was lacking that derives from, as well as reflects, intense emotional bonds. While preoccupied with making new starts in life, however, her parents had not let go of each other completely, and Gail could therefore not help becoming involved in her parents' ambivalence over their own separation.

CONFLICTS UNDER THE MODE OF BINDING

Neither the father nor the mother seemed unduly intent on binding Gail. I noticed, however, that the mother at times bound Gail on the elementary-dependency level by overtly and regressively gratifying the girl. For example, she would suddenly present her with expensive gifts or give into wishes of Gail's that seemed extravagant. Such sporadic yet inconsistent overpermissiveness on the part of the mother, I realized, essentially served to cover up her rejection of the girl, a rejection that seemed only too understandable in the light of her own experiences and needs. Typically, Mrs. Dixon seemed torn between condemning, scolding, and rebuffing Gail, and overgratifying and spoiling her. Some of Gail's cynicism seemed to reflect her awareness of the inconsistency and falsity of her mother's "givingness." Also, Mrs. Dixon often bribed Gail into helping at home, as she frequently needed a sitter for the younger children.

CONFLICTS UNDER THE MODE OF DELEGATING

To some extent, both parents used Gail as a delegate. Particularly when she felt empty and despondent, the mother needed Gail to provide excitement in the manner alluded to earlier. Herself starved for sexually and affectively gratifying relationships, she would then spy on, and hassle over, Gail's correspondence and "affairs" in a manner which provided covert encouragement to Gail and, at the same time, allowed the mother to share in Gail's affairs.

Moreover, Mrs. Dixon, no less than Mr. Dixon, tried to woo Gail as an ally in the ongoing marital war. At the time of our contact with the family, Mr. Dixon was more successful in winning Gail as an ally. Whenever he could, he tried to encourage Gail to act in ways that would displease and inconvenience his wife. For example, at a point when the mother seemed to have the greatest stake in keeping Gail hospitalized, because she was eager to enter her new business venture and could not afford a quarrelsome, defiant daughter at home, he helped to engineer the girl's runaway from the hospital.

CONFLICTS UNDER THE MODE OF EXPELLING

The more I saw this family, the more the neglecting and rejecting attitudes of both parents came to the fore. Not only did the mother attribute to Gail negative qualities such as dishonesty, trickiness, defiance, unreliability, etc., but she also, from very early on, tended to define Gail as unusually precocious and independent. She described Gail as her little "self-sufficient shadow." She allowed her to go out and buy her own lunch at a local lunch counter at age four. While she thus pushed the girl into premature self-sufficiency, she rationalized her neglect and deprivation of Gail as concern for the girl's autonomy. (Similarly, she "trained" Gail's two younger brothers for early autonomy, with the result that they—now seven and nine years respectively—usually get up by themselves, prepare their own breakfast, and march off to school while their mother sleeps until late in the morning.)

The mother's rejection of Gail became even more apparent after Gail's hospital treatment ended. The parents continued for a while in couple therapy. With Gail out of sight, the mother, and to a lesser degree the father, appeared freer to express their conviction that Gail essentially was a nuisance and a troublemaker. The mother could even admit to herself and the therapist that Gail was a liability to her. Not surprisingly, to the extent that she could thus more freely acknowledge her hostile and rejecting feelings toward Gail, her relationship with the girl seemed to improve. For a while, at least, Gail and her mother could live together under one roof with less hassling than had seemed possible before.

As is typical of many expelled adolescents, Gail's conflicts over separation appeared shallow or displaced. In disengaging herself early from her family, she tended to externalize and partially reenact with "boyfriends," probation officers, and therapists those preoedipal and oedipal conflicts which more bound and delegated adolescents tend to struggle through with their parents. At the same time, she directed to these people unsatisfied nurturant needs which then threatened to engulf her in torrents of primitive ambivalence. As a consequence, she quickly had to flee these promising but feared relations. Her displaced separation conflicts thus were aborted, as none of her extraparental relations allowed for sufficient commitment, depth, or complexity. This had major implications for her growth, a topic which shall occupy us in the next chapter.

6

Vicissitudes of Adolescent Growth and Separation

To assess growth in the adolescent, we must examine the quality of his relationships and of his conflicts. Both interweave and both reflect, as well as affect, his growth. Of his relationships, we ask: Do they enrich or impoverish him, and do they correct or worsen the damage caused by earlier relationships? And of his conflicts—be these intrapsychic or interpersonal—we ask: Do they make him stronger, more mature, and autonomous, or do they leave him crushed, weakened, or arrested? I shall reflect on these questions by relating adolescent growth to the previously described transactional modes.

ADOLESCENT GROWTH WITHIN THE BINDING MODE

This mode makes the balance of the adolescent's peer and parent relationships lopsided. It militates against peer relations while it favors, i.e., intensifies and prolongs, his relations with his parents. For bound adolescents, we saw, tend to avoid peers.

Their peer avoidance reflects the type of binding—affective, cognitive, or loyalty binding—that prevails.

Affectively bound adolescents are often spoiled kids because they are used to having things served on a platter by their parents. Therefore, they are quickly disappointed and are easily teased and rebuffed by their peers. For them they embody now those childish and regressive temptations which they try to fight in themselves. Consequently, most affectively bound adolescents quickly reclaim the parental orbit where they can feel accepted albeit hassled.

Cognitively bound adolescents (such as Max, described in Chapter 4) are even more likely to come to grief with peers. For they are headed for a "culture shock"—proportionate to the gap that exists between their family and peer cultures. When they timidly venture into the peer world, they become frightened and painfully self-conscious. Many of the skills they learned—perceptive, language, and motor skills—and many of their basic assumptions seem now bewilderingly out of place. In seeking new relations, i.e., in seeking a new self-revelation and self-confirmation with and through others, they court disaster. Hence, these adolescents, too, pull back to the parental orbit.

So do, finally, those loyalty-bound adolescents whose rueful return to their parents often includes self-destruction and atonement, as I have shown.

To the extent that his peer world recedes, that of the adolescent's parents gains importance. His boundness to them, we notice here, paradoxically causes his conflicts to intensify *as well as* to blur. They intensify because he has no objects other than his parents. His whole relational drama is played out with them alone. It is as if he were locked with them into an incestuous hothouse where ambivalences cannot but stir fiercely.

But while his conflicts intensify, they are also often—particularly when he is cognitively bound—muted. For where an articulate separateness of positions and boundaries is lacking, the protagonists communicate on elusive primary process wavelengths, and conflicts get blurred. Such blurring of conflicts may foster a heightened "consensus sensitivity," including a certain emotional "tuning-in" capacity for spotting danger signals in overpoweringly intrusive parents, but it leaves little room for growth that involves individuation and autonomy.

In assessing growth, we must not only consider the quality of conflicts in general, but also of specific "conflict solutions." Conflicts within the binding mode may "resolve" in certain typical ways which differently affect the adolescent's growth.

One possible "conflict solution" here is the dramatic expulsion, as earlier described. The heightened ambivalence and sense of being caged in (experienced by all parties) engender an expelling momentum that finally breaks the centripetal deadlock. Such dramatic expulsions, we saw, may climax a binding (or delegating) mode and may become definitive. When this happens, the adolescent's pain and hurt can be bitter, but may presage further growth. With the doors to his family locked behind him, he can venture into new relations and learning and eventually can relate to his parents from a position of tested autonomy.

Where, in contrast, the bound adolescent remains centripetally deadlocked, his potential for growth decreases. But even here chances for growth remain as long as conflicts stay alive, i.e., as long as he struggles with his parents and himself, fumbling, misdirected, and undefined as these struggles may appear. (As a therapist, I always feel hopeful when there are signs of conflict and painful struggle. Such signs, I believe, are always prognostically more favorable than early assurances of trust and cooperativeness.)

The chances for growth fade when conflicts, instead of being kept alive, are enduringly avoided or aborted. Within the binding mode, this happens in three main ways. First, the adolescent, weary of struggling, may mold his character so as to turn into a "good," submissive and compliant fellow. Staying infantilized, then, becomes his way of life, as happens with many affectively bound adolescents. The tiger who could terrify his parents through his wild tantrums and demands is now tamed. He grows fat and eats out of his parents'—or their substitutes'—hands.

Or the bound adolescent, beset by unbearable conflict and ambivalence, may try to enduringly numb out any awareness of inner strain. Max, described in Chapter 4, did just this when, blocked from reading "heavy" books and from entering his peer group, he numbed himself with the help of rock music and television commercials. (Other adolescents try to achieve the same result by seeking heavy psychedelic drug effects.)

Finally, when infantile compliance and numbing are not enough, the bound adolescent may enduringly retreat into a fantasy world. Through such retreat, he hopes to survive in a niche even though he remains bodily close to his tangled, suffocating family.

All these attempts to avoid or abort conflicts, though, bode poorly for this adolescent's growth, as becomes clearer when we contrast the bound adolescent's plight with that of his delegated and expelled age mates.

ADOLESCENT GROWTH WITHIN
THE DELEGATING MODE

As a rule, the delegate's relations and conflicts with his parents are less squelching than those of bound adolescents. Therefore, they leave room for a wider development of differentiated skills and motivations and for—not seldom dramatic —shifts in the partners' positions and contributions.

The adolescent who tries to execute his delegated mission(s) *can and must move actively into the peer group,* and this fact, above others, makes his conflicts and chances of growth different from those of the (primarily) bound adolescents.

Whereas "bound" adolescents tend to avoid peers (even though they may join them half-heartedly and abortively), delegated adolescents *seek* peers (or alternate adults) with their parents' covert or overt consent (although, like good retriever dogs, they must report back to these parents). Therefore, the delegated adolescent can find in his peers outlets for his intensifying aggressive and libidinal drives. His relations can diversify, he meets other objects than his parents, and in general is less ambivalently entrapped by them.

However, certain types of conflicts with his parents, such as the earlier-described conflicts of missions and loyalties, are bound to intensify, at least for a while. This happens, for example, when a delegate must provide his parent (or parents) with vicarious thrills and, at the same time, must embody their virtuous ego ideal (e.g., become a precocious sex athlete and also study for the ministry); or when he, in fulfilling his father's unrealized ambitions, must rise above his father and, at the same time, must allow his father to see himself as the most successful man in the family—i.e., must stay below his father.

Such conflicts may deeply pain and even crush the adolescent. Still, his chances for growth—that is, for his final gain of insight, humanity, and strength—are in general good. To understand this, we must further examine the delegate's separation conflicts and must look at how he ventures into the peer world.

His ventures into the peer world, although sanctioned by his parents, eventually confront them with risks. As much as they might believe him in their grip, such grip is threatened once his peers present alternative life experiences, models, and values. He now gets the taste of liberation—similar to those blacks who, made aware of alternatives to oppression, demand more freedom and equality the very moment their lot improves. We may speak of an accelerating liberating momentum. The adolescent's new cognitive cleverness, described earlier, increases his discriminating perceptions and awareness of alternative experiences and models. Once outside the family orbit, he can more imaginatively map out action courses that foster his eventual separation.

The more he separates, the more "objectively" he can see his parents, his relationship to them, and the missions entrusted to him. At the same time, he can see them as more conflicted, needful, and weaker than he believed they were and, perhaps more importantly, can view them as being torn by *their* developmental crisis. As a result, he understands more easily that they need to exploit him as delegate.

Such insight may dramatically change the balance of psychological power. By delineating his parents as vulnerable, conflicted, and weak—i.e., by lambasting them as cowards, squares, or establishment types—he gains new leverage to hurt them. In the terms of Hegel's master–slave paradigm, the slave gains and the master loses power.

But, and herewith emerges a further level of drama and complexity, the adolescent's gain of power can also delay and seemingly thwart his separation, as it increases his anxiety and guilt. He now feels anxious because more than before he must live by his own resources, must "own" the anguish of his ambivalence and uncertainty (instead of projecting it on others), and must confront envy and competition from peers. He feels guilty because he betrays his loyalty as a delegate. His guilt, like that of the seriously bound adolescents, may cause him to flounder under signs of turmoil, agony, and possibly self-destruction. It may then seem that he cannot escape his parents' leash. But, unlike the pervasively bound-up adolescent, the "straying" delegate usually reclaims his foot-hold in the world of peers even though his parents, exploiting his loyalty, may resort to ever more massively binding maneuvers, thereby—for a while at least—intensifying the separation struggle. It is then, after all, in this very struggle (to be elaborated later) that he, along with his parents, can grow.

Gary illustrates such a drama of growth and separation in an adolescent delegate. I introduced Gary earlier as a sixteen-year-old boy whose father had delegated him to satisfy belatedly his own wanderlust. Here I shall focus on Gary's relationship to his mother, who expected him to serve her in four main functions—two of which reflected a predominantly binding, and two a delegating mode.

First, Gary was bound as the recipient of his mother's disowned and externalized emptiness and depression. It was only after many months of family and couple therapy that her depressive emptiness, manifested in a life of self-sacrificing suburban drudgery, sans joy and sans hope, fully emerged.

Typically, for a long time she could not speak of her *own* depression and emptiness, but could only lament Gary's depression—selectively disregarding in him all signs of liberative initiative and self-enjoyment.

Second, Gary had to absorb his mother's infantilizing and eroticizing pressures, pressures which built up as a result of unsatisfying relations with her parents and husband. Not surprisingly, he experienced strong homosexual and passive urges. Also, he avoided peers who posed competitive threats and masculine challenges. Instead, he established "special" relationships with certain older people, such as art teachers and ministers, who served him as parent substitutes.

But—and herewith we turn to the third function, which we can properly call a mission—such peer avoidance, fostered by the mother's binding, was at odds with her demands that Gary bring young people and young life into her home. He had to associate with stimulating friends who would alleviate her drudgery and would provide the adolescent excitement she herself had missed. In order that he could here serve as her delegate, Gary, albeit conditionally, had to seek the peer group.

Finally, a fourth major function complemented the third, just mentioned, and created a further centrifugal push. It related to his mother's ego ideal. Years ago she had given up her own strong professional ambitions when she took care of her chronically decrepit parents who, by *their* loyalty-binding stratagems, had extracted her sacrifice. She subsequently married a man who extracted a similar sacrifice, and she therefore channeled onto Gary her immense, unfulfilled aspirations. Gary initially held out the promise that he would realize them, as he was bright, handsome, affable, and artistic. She made him cultivate his talents and tried to turn him into a genius who would fulfill her dreams.

The point arrived, however, when Gary broke down under these conflicting expectations. He was then thirteen years old. After having been his mother's delight in the form of a handsome, tender, promising, superachieving student, he now became depressed, obstreperous, and ran away. He lost interest in his schoolwork with the sole exception of art lessons. He was torn between avoiding and seeking peers, longed for their friendships but feared their competitive bantering. He craved special attention but withdrew when he met with rebuff. The more he became stymied in depressive idleness, the more his mother worried. The more she worried, the more she pressured him with contradictory messages. She conveyed to him that she wanted him as he *had* been, docile, charming, handsome; and not as he was now, sullen, conflicted, defiant, pimpled, and running around with "bums." She told him to move out into the world, to work harder, and to become a paragon of early independence; and she also told him to stay with her and make her life meaningful. While giving these conflicting messages, she thought of him, so she told him and me, day and night, thus impressing on him how her own emotional and physical survival depended on him alone.

In this situation, Gary realized more clearly his own importance to his mother (and, though for somewhat different reasons, to his father). Also, while gaining a foothold in the peer world—precarious as it was—he realized his parents' own conflicts and weaknesses. With that, the balance of psychological power tipped to his side. Enraged over his exploitation by his parents, he ripped into them, denounced them as restricted, conventional squares hung up on obsolete values, and accused them of wrecking his life. The parents seemed devastated and stunned. But the more they reeled in confusion, conflict, and hurt, the more Gary's indignation waned. He floundered, sulked, and failed in his academic work as well as in his relations to peers. As if under an unconscious compulsion, he turned himself into a target for their righteous wrath. Defeating himself, he attested his need to atone for his rise in psychological power and for his centrifugal stirrings.

However, though Gary thus slipped back into his parents' leash, he was nonetheless winning ground. He slipped only temporarily, as it turned out. Assisted by his individual therapy, he resumed the centrifugal push. A year later Gary still struggled with many problems, yet was settled in school, worked diligently in a part-time job, and continued to move into a group of peers—male and female—that was congenial to him.

ADOLESCENT GROWTH WITHIN
THE EXPELLING MODE

Here again we must examine this adolescent's interweaving relationships and conflicts, as these are colored by the strong centrifugal push and pull of the expelling mode.

Being rejected and neglected by his parents, the expellee must seek his salvation in the peer group and outside world. He is pushed into premature autonomy. This relational trend contrasts with that found in the binding mode, where parent relationships gain and peer relationships lose in importance.

But although shallow and attenuated, his relations with his parents are not devoid of conflict. In fact, conflicts with them can be hateful and cutting. This seeming paradox is resolved when we realize that the attenuation of the parental bond does not only bring respite from massively reactivated oedipal and preoedipal entanglements; it also deprives the adolescent of the chance to grow through parent-related conflicts and, even more important, to grow through the experience of a tender and caring intimacy. This means he will lack those capacities and skills which thrive on caring and intimate, though possibly conflicted, relationships. Therefore, his capacity to differentiate and perceive subtle feelings, to experience empathy, to delay gratification, and to modulate and subordinate his own interpersonal behavior to long-range goals and to rewards remains blunted. Having lacked intimate and caring experiences with his parents, this adolescent's libidinal and aggressive drives are likely to break through abruptly and preemptorily, making his attacks appear brutal and callous. This minimizes his chances for experiencing even belatedly the kind of intimate and caring relationships which he missed.

My observations on expellees (among them many "casual" runaways) who were exposed to insidious parental neglect and rejection confirmed such expectations. Among these expellees I found typically those tough, delinquent adolescents who, in stark contrast to the inhibited and bound adolescents described earlier, had no qualms about "taking" and discarding girls, and about attacking others casually and wantonly. They attacked members of their own gang as easily as they attacked outsiders, authority figures, or cars and schoolroom windows.

Stunting of growth is revealed also when we focus on the maturation of cognitive skills, which I described as a major feature of adolescence. We observe in the expellee, as we did in the bound adolescent, a characteristic "perverted" use of reasoning. But the quality is different in each case. In bound children, reasoning seems "perverted" in the sense that it contributes to the ongoing mystification and dependent entanglement of these children. In many tough expellees, such perversion of cognition is revealed in manipulative cunning.

Cunning becomes here a weapon in a struggle wherein it is less important to utilize and integrate the data and observations others can offer, than to use such data selectively in order to assert one's independence, to establish distance, and to put the other down. Maturation, in other words, is not used to enrich one's interpersonal relations and to facilitate cooperative, sharing endeavors; instead, it is mainly used to outwit and fight the other and to maneuver him into a position where he cannot pose threats.

The implications of such a power struggle for the expellee's growth and separation become even clearer when we consider the third, earlier mentioned, feature of adolescence: the required shift and modification of loyalties. I have described how binding and delegating parents interfere with their children's transfer of loyalties. Instead of helping their children with such transfer, these parents nourish an excessive loyalty which ties the adolescents more closely to them and turns them, if so desired, into reliable, efficient delegates. In the expelling mode, the opposite holds true. For this mode lacks the kind of ongoing parental investment in the child which marks the two other modes. As these parents neglect and reject their children, they do not seem to care whether the latter are loyal to them or not. Thus, they fail to build that bond which, in extreme cases, can turn the child into a lifelong self-sacrificing victim adjunct. Therefore, the rejected and neglected children do not appear weighed down by loyalty burdens. They appear footloose, and therefore can easily separate from parents who do not care. But what from one angle appears an asset, the ease with which they can separate and move into new relationships, turns into a liability when we look for depth, commitment, and caring in human relations, qualities of growth that are lacking in the relationships of expellees.

When an expelled adolescent separates, he knows it is for him a matter of sinking or swimming. But unlike the bound and delegated adolescent, he has been trained early to make it on his own. He has been trained to live in a human jungle wherein people do not care, where they try to outwit and manipulate each other, and where relations are shallow and exploitative. In moving away from home early and in moving into the peer group easily, he carries with him a world view and life style that may not appeal to many but are the only ones he knows.*

* A comparison with the Mafia seems appropriate. In the Mafia we find much delinquent toughness, but also—and this seems to indicate a difference from the delinquents here described—a certain (misplaced) loyalty. Many reports indicate that certain types of loyalties are strong and can be exploited. For example, certain Mafia members are easily directed to kill other members primarily because they feel loyalty toward a certain ingroup or boss. We find here, I believe, elements of the Italian family wherein the binding and delegating of children, and hence the instilling of a strong sense of loyalty, seems to go together with a lack of *loyalty* toward public authorities and entities such as the government, community, etc. Many delinquent gangs also reveal strong loyalty phenomena of one sort or another. These phenomena deserve further examination. We may ask: Do these loyalty phenomena—for example, the loyalty of gang members toward the gang leader—reflect reparative phenomena, that is, a belated maturation of interpersonal attitudes on which these children missed out, or are these phenomena indications of family constellations wherein strong binding and delegating elements existed side by side with expelling ones?

PART
II

7

Separation Dynamics in Schizophrenia

Elsewhere I have written on schizophrenia as a disturbance that is controversial, complex, and difficult to fathom (see Stierlin, 1965, 1967, 1969, 1972a). Here I limit my objectives. I shall view some forms of this disturbance as paradigms of extreme human conditions or *"Grenzsituationen,"* which, according to K. Jaspers, reveal the bounds of human existence. We focus on an extraordinary drama of relationships which puts the ordinary in perspective, a drama that reveals severe transactional mode disturbances.

TRANSACTIONAL MODES IN THE ORDINARY SEPARATION PROCESS

As a first step, we must widen the scope of these modes. We must ask, what place do the modes of binding, delegating, and expelling have in the ordinary separation process? To what extent do they reflect normal or pathological phenomena?*

---

* Human psychopathology, from the position here adopted, always reflects a predisposition which interacts with its human environment. In order to classify psychopathology, we must, first, determine what is salient in this pre-

To answer these questions, we must take a long-range view of the separation process.

This separation process can be conceived as a gradually expanding spiral of mutual individuation and differentiation which, increasingly, leads to both parties' relative independence. This process lasts through the child's infancy, adolescence, and early adulthood. Such a long-range view of the process makes us realize that parental binding, delegating, and expelling find therein a legitimate place—up to a point. These modes become exploitative and damaging to the child when they are inappropriately timed, mixed, or excessively intense. Let us, first, consider how elements of these modes seem appropriate to certain phases of the separation process.

Some binding seems necessary and legitimate primarily during the early stages of the parent–child intimacy. It conveys to the child his unique importance. Binding, thus understood, is part of the parent's effort to "tame" (*apprivoiser*) the child in the sense in which Antoine de Saint-Exupéry has defined this term in his story of *The Little Prince*. This little prince had to tame the fox in the desert in order to make him his friend and companion. He had to convey to him that he considered him, the fox, uniquely important. In being tamed and bound,

---

disposition (the individual's contribution), salient in the human environment (mainly the parents' contributions), and salient in the interaction of the two (the relational dialectic). In the predisposition we can, for example, consider salient either symptoms or traits such as cognitive and perceptual response dispositions which presumably are enduring. Wynne and Singer (1973a, 1973b) have recently elaborated on these predispositions. In the human environment we can consider as salient the parents' communications as these either encourage or discourage a shared focus of attention (see Wynne and Singer, 1963a, 1963b; Singer and Wynne, 1965a, 1965b). In the interaction we can either (among other things) emphasize how like engenders like, as when, for example, children become like their parents (via identification, imitation, or assimilation); or we can emphasize the generation of differences (as when, for example, children turn passive while responding to actively intrusive parents). In this study, I chose to consider as most salient certain parental transactional styles and certain transactional dynamics.

the fox became *somebody,* he counted, his desert became alive.

However, such binding becomes increasingly inappropriate —that is, exploitative and damaging—when parents continue to direct it toward a child who should learn to test and enjoy his autonomy. And this applies, above all, to the adolescent. An entrenched, unabated parental binding, directed toward an adolescent who should struggle for his autonomy, cannot but become pathogenic.

Similar considerations apply to the delegating mode. Up to a point it seems legitimate for parents to want to enlist their children as delegates. To a degree it seems legitimate that they expect these children to realize their aspirations and ego ideals, to carry on the family name, to remain loyal to their parents, and to bring meaning and satisfaction to their lives. It is particularly during the later stages of childhood—after infancy and before and during adolescence—that legitimate wishes of parents to delegate their children are mobilized. This is the time when the child, more clearly than before, reveals his unique individuality and potentials, when he begins to branch out into the world while he still remains anchored in the family orbit. This is therefore the time when the child, more promisingly than before, offers himself as a potential agent and executor of his parents' wishes and aspirations.

However, delegating parents threaten to exploit and damage their child to the extent that they fail to recognize him as a person in his own right, as one who, in the final analysis, must separate and forge his own destiny. These parents interfere with this task when they, instead of letting him go relatively burden-free, mystify him and weigh him down with their own unresolved conflicts, unfinished repair work, and unfulfilled aspirations.

Also, elements of the expelling mode, we note finally, find a legitimate place in the separation process. Mainly during the later stages of adolescence a certain amount of "benign parental neglect" seems appropriate. Such benign neglect then constitutes the *"vis a tergo"* which provides certain adolescents with that additional push needed to really try it on their own and thereby achieve a decisive new level of a relatively mature independence. Parental rejection and neglect, however, become malignant when they are directed toward a child who still requires nurturant care and executive control and who, instead of needing exposure to the cold winds of autonomy and competition, needs shelter, caring intimacy, and guidance in a bewildering world. From this point of view, the binding and expelling modes have contrasting periods of maximal pathogenicity. Unlike the binding mode, which appears most appropriate and hence least pathogenic during the earliest stage of the parent–child relationship, the expelling mode during this same early phase becomes most malignant and pathogenic, as this is the phase during which the child is most helpless and most dependent on his parents. Those emotionally deprived children whom René Spitz (1945) depicted as victims of hospitalism—children who wither away in apathy and depression despite excellent medical care and hygiene—can be considered victims of an expelling mode that operated malignantly and early.

Within the above long-range view of the separation process, there emerge two life phases which are most critical to schizophrenic development: *early childhood* (spanning approximately the first three and one-half years) and *adolescence*. The first phase I have considered in my work, *Conflict and Reconciliation* (1969); the second is the chief topic of this book. Here, however, although I am most concerned with what happens during adolescence, I cannot completely omit what occurs during the early phase and, indeed, during the whole course of life.

Before we examine schizophrenia under the model of transactional modes, we must briefly review two assumptions. First, we assume that there exists a predisposition—or vulnerability —to later schizophrenia which codetermines the relational dialectic under discussion here. And, second, we assume that this dialectic begins early—perhaps before the infant's birth (because of long-standing maternal fantasies about the as yet unborn child), and certainly long before the period of adolescence.

The most up-to-date research suggests that the predisposition to schizophrenia is relatively weak and unspecific. Like human intelligence, it seems based on different and complexly interacting genes. Yet, albeit weak and unspecific, such a predisposition, from the outset, seems to diminish these individuals' chances to find interpersonal satisfaction, security, and meaning in their lives. These children seem to have less drive, less reconciling strength, and lesser survival assets than other children. They lack what it takes to install and defend solid body boundaries, to focus their attention flexibly as well as directly on others, and hence to tolerate, as well as benefit from, human intimacy. Their initial vulnerability makes them prone to become ever more damaged. Not seldom they suffer birth defects or childhood illnesses that further reduce their adaptive potential. And, perhaps most importantly, they often have to live with parents who, instead of compensating for their vulnerability and traumatization, aggravate their plight.

In accumulative fashion, these parents, by commission and omission, bring their ineptitude to bear on their children.

But—and herewith we turn to the relational dialectic that concerns us—parental ineptitude is not the whole story. In addition to being subjected to parental ineptitude and neglect, many potential schizophrenics are exposed to a more elusive, though no less harmful, damage—that which results from *psychological exploitation*. When we focus on this aspect, we recognize the operation of the transactional modes which I have described. Above all, it is the modes of binding and delegating which seem to determine the fate of the potential schizophrenic. This is because they operate here with excessive intensity and have their main impact at a time when the child is most vulnerable, that is, the time when he is most pliable, dependent, helpless, and therefore most captive to the stronger parent's, particularly the stronger mother's, reality. In order to survive, this child must develop strategies for interpersonal survival which I have described in my *Conflict and Reconciliation* (1969) and elsewhere (1972b). He employs these survival strategies at the expense of his future growth and adaptation. By making himself into a specialist for "symbiotic survival," this child mortgages his interpersonal future. And, as we shall shortly see, much of such mortgage becomes due when he or she enters adolescence—the time that here interests us most.

EXTREMES OF PARENTAL BINDING
LEADING TO SCHIZOPHRENIA

Extremes of parental binding that seem at the root of schizophrenic disturbances have been widely described, although in terms that have varied. Particularly L. Wynne (1963a, b) and M. Singer (1965a, b), W. Brodey (1959), R. Laing (1961, 1965, 1970), D. Ricks and J. Berry (1970), D. Ricks and G. Nameche (1966), R. Scott and P. Ashworth (1965, 1967), R. Scott and A. Montanez (1972), W. Goldfarb (1969), and R. Welldon (1971), have illuminated such dynamics. At this point, I shall only briefly comment on how the previously described varieties of binding—affective, cognitive, and loyalty binding—may become linked to schizophrenia.

Extremes of affective binding, that is, excesses in regressive gratification and infantilization, seem common in children who later become schizophrenic. One of my first schizophrenic patients, a young man of delicate features, until his hospitalization at the age of twenty, was regularly bathed by his mother, always served his choice of food, and infantilized in innumerable ways. Since then, I have seen and read about many similar cases. [Certain mothers of potential schizophrenics, particularly of girls, though, instead of corresponding to the stereotype of the overdoting "Jewish" mother, seem cold and distant, as, among others, T. Lidz (1965) and his collaborators have noted.]

Extremes of cognitive binding, far beyond that described in the preceding chapters, also seem common and fateful. Also here the literature—beginning with G. Bateson's (1956) seminal description of the double bind—is informative. The studies by W. Goldfarb (1962, 1968) and D. Meyers and W. Goldfarb (1962) are especially illuminating. By means of ingenious experiments, these researchers showed how parents of schizophrenic children perplexed and mystified these children to the utmost.

Finally, we notice how many parents imbue their potentially schizophrenic children almost from birth on with a sense of deep and archaic loyalty. From the beginning, they give the message that any joy and meaning experienced apart, and any turning away from, themselves—i.e., from the binding and all-powerful parents—is the child's major crime that cannot but hurt and possibly destroy these parents. Thus, the child's age-appropriate moves toward relative autonomy become in his mind tantamount to murderous aggression directed toward those who "love" him most and whom he believes—or better, is conditioned to believe—that he loves most dearly. This gives rise to the excruciating, though largely unconscious, guilt I have described. Here again some of my earliest experiences with schizophrenic patients provided the most striking examples. I remember how one mother of a patient of mine withdrew into her sickbed when she learned that my patient, then a sixteen-year-old girl, planned to go to summer camp with a friend. Meanwhile, the mother exuded an agonized concern over the dreadful things that might happen to girls at camps, particularly to inexperienced and selfish girls who ignored and mistreated their mothers. Faced with such dire premonitions, my patient promptly canceled the camping venture and, instead, became her mother's nurse.

When parents bind a child simultaneously on the affective, cognitive, and loyalty levels, there ensues mutual thralldom. And the stronger the binding, the more squelching such thralldom becomes. Frequently such a state is termed *symbiosis* or *symbiotic union*. This symbiotic union distorts, exaggerates, and prolongs the normal symbiotic phase of development which M. Mahler (1968) described. It is difficult to convey the oppressive strength of such a pathologic union. "A parent and a child," write D. Ricks and G. Nameche (1966),

form an inseparable unit, prolonged over a long period beyond the usual end of symbiosis [as described by M. Mahler, 1968]. The child is not considered a separate person and boundaries between the parent and child are not recognized. The parent may therefore bathe the child well into adolescence, be so intrusive as to deny the child any privacy in action or thought, and be impervious to any desires that the child expresses in his own right. The child is expected to comply to parental distortions of the environment, physical restraint, and socialized relations . . . the child must remain functionally helpless, have no other close relationships, and not attempt to escape. The record contains no evidence that the child has ever been permitted outside the walls of the home to visit relatives or friends or has ever attended overnight camp.

Typically, the parents of children in symbiotic union, as described by D. Ricks and G. Nameche (1966), appear stalemated in extreme centripetal relations. Many of these parents seem to "neutralize" their murderous rage and frustration (felt mainly toward each other) by staking out a precarious "parallel marital life." Other authors—such as M. Bowen (1961, 1965, 1966), and T. Lidz, et al. (1957)—use the terms "emotional divorce" or "marital schism" to describe this pattern of marital deadlock.

The available evidence, particularly as presented by Ricks and Nameche, suggests that schizophrenic patients growing up in symbiotic union (with a disturbed parent who lives emotionally divorced from his spouse) have the poorest prognosis of all schizophrenics as far as remissions and releases from a hospital are concerned. Hence they seem the most likely candidates to fill the back wards of psychiatric institutions. In the light of the above considerations, this is to be expected. For excessive binding, operating on all three levels, cannot but train the child to become a chronic, immobilized recipient of care—to be doled out either at home or in an institution.

EXTREMES OF PARENTAL DELEGATING
LEADING TO SCHIZOPHRENIA

In addition to, and interweaving with, maximal binding, delegating, when extreme, may give rise to schizophrenic disturbances. Such schizophrenic disturbances can be expected to differ, however, in phenomenology and prognosis from those where excessive binding operates. Delegated patients who become schizophrenic are torn asunder by conflicts of missions and loyalties. Yet they can be expected to have a better long-term prognosis than more pervasively bound patients. For these delegated schizophrenic patients, even though gripped by conflicting loyalties and missions, can get a foothold in the world of peers and alternate adults and can thus promote their final liberation. We can expect them to become acutely, rather than chronically, disturbed, and to be released at least on and off from psychiatric institutions. My own—mainly psychotherapeutic—experiences with schizophrenic patients and their families bear this out, as does the research which G. Nameche, et al. (1964), R. Scott and A. Montanez (1972), and others report.

In order to fathom the intensity of conflicts and stresses to which such delegates can be subjected, we must reflect on the missions they are expected to fulfill. Many of these missions imply extreme demands, made on the delegate and his reconciling capacity, and seem incompatible with what his age and ordinary adaptation would require.

Several "missions impossible" particularly stand out here, such as, first of all, the mission to destroy one parent out of loyalty to the other—the mission for which Hamlet, hovering on the brink of a schizophrenic breakdown, provided the classic paradigm.

We must mention, second, the mission to embody and actualize a parent's grandiose ego ideal. The more such a parent senses that he or she cannot realize this ideal alone, the more desperately he or she turns to the child for salvation. This child, of only average endowment, must reach dizzying heights of achievement and fame and must share these willingly with the delegating parent. In other cases, he might have to embody all the beauty and vitality which this parent feels lacking or wanting in him- or herself.

Third, and this is the perhaps most fateful mission, such a delegate might become recruited to embody and externalize the badness and craziness which a parent, in his innermost self, feels and fears to be his fate. This child must then serve his parent's self-observation, as earlier described. Living under the (disowned) threat and spell of madness, such a parent seems often impelled to search for—and, in the process, create—madness in the child. Often such parental fear of, and concern with, madness seems understandable. R. Scott and P. Ashworth (1969), particularly, have shown that parents who unwittingly seek and implant madness in their children are often haunted by the shadows of mad relatives or ancestors. Hence, they grow up with the notion and expectation, frightening beyond comprehension, that madness again will strike their tainted family. It is then in the attempt to control, contain, and neutralize this feared and ever-present madness that a child becomes delegated to enact it, that is, becomes the mad family member.

VICISSITUDES OF EXTREME BINDING IN ADOLESCENCE

Adolescence hastens the day of reckoning for child and parent. It brings the generations to a crisis point at which there unfolds the drama of centrifugal and centripetal forces, of push and pull, of attempted individuation and separation, of mutual hurt and reconciliation that is the subject of this book. Let us now briefly consider how this drama develops when potential schizophrenics, while being propelled into adulthood, become subject to extreme binding and delegating.

Extreme Binding

The maximally bound and potentially schizophrenic adolescent, it follows from the above, clings to what an outsider perceives as sickness, thralldom, and misery. In so doing, he defies psychological logic—and the imperatives of survival. He forfeits whatever chances for growth and liberation he has. He remains tied to the parent's emotional orbit as if held by an iron band. He is a self-sacrificing, willing victim, an Isaac who stubbornly carries the knife that will slaughter him.

Such is, indeed, the way certain schizophrenic patients impress me. With unwavering determination, they cling to a parent or parents whose every move, contrary to these parents' conscious intentions, appear to abet their child's destruction. Scott and Ashworth (1969) and Welldon (1971) described this phenomenon. Welldon presented portraits of four families with a hospitalized schizophrenic member who was extremely bound.

One of Welldon's patients is Betty. It is her extreme boundness and determination to cling to a destructive family orbit that strikes the observer. All family members reflect and reinforce such boundness and all members resist fiercely any therapeutic intervention that might liberate them. We read that:

The more successful the nursing staff became in their treatment of Betty, the greater the competition and the less tolerable the mutual anger between ourselves [i.e., the therapists] and the family, and in particular with mother, became. We gave up after six sessions. Though we had gained new insight, this seemed to make the task of therapy more, rather than less, difficult. Mother, with her rigid and paranoid defenses, was impervious to change. She needed Betty to be ill in order that she should nurse her. She was convinced that Betty would never be cured, and she knew that when she died Betty would have to be put in a mental hospital. "So why can't I have her now?" She continually expressed the fear that the worst would happen, that while Betty was in the hospital something would go wrong—she would catch pneumonia or be attacked by a male patient. Father and brother, too, were caught up in this web of smothering and expiating overprotection. Mother once admitted, "What else can I do? This is the only way I know of loving Betty." The more effectively the hospital staff treated Betty, the more strongly the rest of the family had to deny any improvement and to set up an underground resistance to restore the family status quo in which Betty played so crucial and sacrificial a part.

Another schizophrenic girl in Dr. Welldon's sample is Janet. She had spent the last six of her twenty-three years deteriorating in a mental hospital. When Dr. Welldon saw her the first time, she screamed at him and ran off. She "resembled an animal in a cage, frightened and frustrated, hopeless and helpless in her isolation, emanating a feeling of danger to herself and to others." Janet became physically ill at a point when the parents in their therapeutic sessions began to reveal openly some of their intense frustration and misery. She then died slowly of hypostatic bronchopneumonia. Thus "it seemed as if Janet were fulfilling her own and her parents' prophecies, as if she were the guardian of some fearful, unintelligible secret that could not be divulged."

In reflecting on the meaning of Janet's death, Dr. Welldon wondered whether he had witnessed—and possibly speeded up—"some malignant family process involving the extrusion of Janet that had been operating for a long time." Thus he suggests that severely bound schizophrenics may also, paradoxically, become definitively expelled. It is this seeming paradox which brings into view an extreme dynamic of separation which requires further reflection.

In order to understand this dynamic, we must remind ourselves that extreme binding may trigger explosive expulsions. Yet we must also remind ourselves that here the parent–child relationship is such that neither a state of extreme boundness nor one of definitive expulsion seems viable for parent or child. Hence a compromise needs to be worked out and it is this compromise that can look like a paradox. We are indebted to Scott and Ashworth (1967) for having illuminated this situation.

"In a hypothetically pure symbiosis," Scott and Ashworth reflect, "the two partners do not relate and they cannot separate. They have to be 'identical' or they split totally apart. They are 'totally in' or 'totally out.' " Yet, the authors proceed to show, there can occur a dramatic event which can change the quality of the symbiotic union and can "disconnect" the partners. This event they call "closure" and, within our conceptual framework, it can be viewed as a form of dramatic expulsion. This closure, or dramatic expulsion, implies that the patient—i.e., ordinarily an adolescent offspring—comes to be perceived as " 'ill,' mad, beyond human influence or concern," that he is condemned to a living death—a shadow existence to be led in a mental hospital. But—and this highlights the seeming paradox—this "dead" patient, condemned to live in a shadowy Hades, retains the power to fill his parents' lives with never-ending terror, concern, and guilt. The patient's dead body, although removed from the home, remains available for continuous ritualistic observances. Thus, unlike the dead described by Virgil and Dante who fear (and perhaps relish) being forgotten, many living dead, who are called chronic schizophrenics, are refused Lethe's drink: Although maximally alienated, they stay yet maximally bound to their parents.

Scott and Ashworth have perceptively traced how "closure" comes about. "When the 'child' first breaks down," we learn, "he becomes as a rule the center of a peculiarly intense parental awareness. He becomes the object of parental scrutiny, usually silent and oblique," while "conflict between the parents, often deep and unresolvable, now invariably takes place through the patient to a greater extent than before." At this point many psychiatrists become agents in sealing for good such closure.* They spell out and hence officially sanction a "diagnosis" and sentence of "mental illness." But even with such official help the parents have gained little respite from their misery. For these parents, the authors note sympathetically, after having engineered closure with a colluding—i.e., bound-up—patient, bind themselves ever more deeply and tragically.

From the time of the first breakdown these parents sacrifice their own lives for the patient in ritualistic form. In the ritual they "do it all for the patient"; there is a total and real denial of their own needs and satisfactions. "I only want what he wants," they say.

---

* This agent role of the psychiatrist deserves critical reflection. Typically, the psychiatrist is brought into the picture when parents, after varying periods of agony and ambivalence, are about to dramatically expel their child. These parents then try to enlist his help to tip their ambivalence definitively. They recruit him as a surgeon who is expected to diagnose and cut off the bad, gangrenous "family flesh," to effect its radical sequestration and expulsion. They expect this psychiatrist to label the patient as sick and in need of institutionalization. By giving official medical approval, he has to sanction the rejecting side of the parents' ambivalence and relieve their guilt about expelling their child.

Such a psychiatrist is placed at a critical juncture in the patient's and family's life. He can use his influence to keep the potential expellee within the family orbit and, in so doing, can try to redistribute to the family the patient's badness and symptoms, that is, he can try to keep alive and "workable" the parents' ambivalence; or he can, by the power of his authority, provide the definitive, expelling push.

No longer able to allow themselves any life of their own, they make the patient the grave of all their own hopes and desires.

Extreme Binding and Running Away

We can further clarify the separation dynamics of potentially schizophrenic patients by once more considering the runaway picture. We found extreme binding to be at odds with running away, as extremely bound adolescents—and among them many schizophrenics—ordinarily have neither the will nor the ability to run to peers. Also, their inordinate guilt about running away from home—i.e., their guilt over committing the number-one crime—usually sabotages a runaway success. In addition, we find certain unusual runaway ventures or "runaway extremes."

One such "runaway extreme" is represented by lonely schizoid runaways, of whom Roy, described in Chapter 2, is an example. Roy, hospitalized for many months with a diagnosis of schizophrenia, ran away repeatedly from his home and later from his hospital. To an outsider, his runaway ventures seemed unmotivated, bizarre, lonely, and risky, as he strayed in alleys or empty churchyards and made himself conspicuous to strangers and policemen. He was killed during his last runaway episode, when his sleeping bag, placed close to the edge of a country road, was hit by a speeding car. From my knowledge of Roy and his family, I had little doubt that he courted death to appease his excruciating "breakaway guilt."

A second extreme form of running away—or runaway equivalent—may be called "running away inwards," to use a term suggested by L. Wynne (1971). Here the patient does not run away bodily, only psychologically, as he entrenches himself in a world of fantasies and inner objects, beside whose lure the world of living creatures fades. By "running away inwards," he seems to loosen his bind to his powerful parents, without really succeeding. For if we scrutinize his fantasies and inner world—as we have done over months and years of individual and family therapy—we find the bind operating *in* and *through* this inner world. For we find then his fantasies to interweave complexly with those of his parents in what I. Boszormenyi-Nagy (1965, 1966) has called "intersubjective fusion." Thus, in the final analysis, running away inwardly is hardly less illusionary and self-defeating than the actual lonely running away of boys like Roy.

Finally, any hospitalization in a mental institution can be viewed as a runaway attempt in which parents and patient often collude and which, very likely, will fail due to the parties' continuing tragic boundness to each other.

THE INTERPLAY OF BINDING AND DELEGATING IN
THE SEPARATION EFFORT OF
POTENTIAL SCHIZOPHRENICS

While binding is crucial in the development of schizophrenia, delegating, too, is important. However, the situation and prognosis for the participants differs under these two modes. Depending on the strength of the loyalty bond, the nature of his mission and the type or intensity of dilemmas to which he is exposed, any delegate cannot but suffer deep conflict and turmoil when he tries to separate. Often this turmoil will have the features of an acute schizophrenic break. But because he has acquired more interpersonal skills and can make available to himself models and values which allow further (though limited) separation and individuation, he seems less in danger of becoming chronically schizophrenic than the severely bound child.

In actual life, the binding (which may lead to dramatic expulsion or closure) *and* delegating of the potential schizophrenic tend to occur together. It is the relative strength of the binding versus the delegating forces which determines whether and how schizophrenia, or a state labeled as schizophrenia, ensues. To illustrate such interactions of the binding and delegating modes, I shall conclude this chapter by briefly describing a family with several children who are potential schizophrenics.

The Smith family, whom I had a chance to treat and observe for a period of a year and a half, consisted of the parents, both in their mid-forties, and six children of whom two—both girls, fifteen and nineteen years, respectively—were seen in family and individual therapy. A seventeen-year-old brother lived in a distant hippie community. Three younger children below the age of twelve still lived at home. Each of the older three children had been a runaway. It was their runaway ventures which, more than other features, illustrated the binding and delegating modes that bore on their schizophrenic developments. I shall focus mainly on how these modes appeared in Cindy, fifteen years old when I saw her.

Cindy, looking like a Della Robbia angel who had turned tramp, was admitted to a psychiatric hospital after a lengthy runaway episode in which she had gone as far away as Oregon. While on the road, she had taken numerous drugs, "freaked out" on several LSD trips, been gang-banged, jailed, and contracted lice. When admitted to the ward, she appeared washed out, vague and depressed, and troubled by feelings that everything—and particularly her body—was unreal and "freaky." A detailed diagnostic interview revealed that many "crazy and funny things" were going on inside her mind and body; but none of these experiences seemed clear-cut and blatant enough to warrant a diagnosis of actual schizophrenia. Before she ran away, her schoolwork had deteriorated. Increasingly, she had skipped classes and had been disorderly. This aroused her father's ire; he lambasted her as a slut and drifter, finally (according to Cindy) forcing her to run away with a girlfriend who seemed no less troubled and unhappy than she was.

Cindy had certain capacities and motivations for relating to peers and had, in fact, mastered some impressive survival skills which had allowed her to get away as far as Oregon. She differed therefore from those severely bound adolescents who either cannot run away at all, can only run away inwardly, or can run away only abortively.

As I got to know Cindy and her family, I was impressed by the strength and complexity of the binding and delegating modes that operated on her. These modes originated from her parents. Neither parent was healthy. Mr. Smith, a banker of Irish descent, looked wiry but suffered from high blood pressure, stomach cramps, sudden bouts of diarrhea, and other somatic troubles which, off and on, kept him incapacitated for hours or days. Mrs. Smith, originally a teacher, was grossly overweight because she stopped taking her thyroid pills after she found out that her children had been stealing them in order to get "high." Both parents drank a lot to dilute the rage, frustration, and unhappiness engendered by a marriage which had grown unbearable; and they both struggled with burdens from their pasts.

Mr. Smith, a suspicious and lonely man, had been deceived and deprived by his poor immigrant parents. As a young man, he had a fling at a promiscuous and adventurous life which was cut short when, in his early twenties, he married Mrs. Smith, whose wealth, erudition, and seeming maternal givingness attracted him. However, the two were soon deadlocked in their unmet needs. For Mrs. Smith, far from being the giving "teacher mother" he had expected her to be, was at heart a greedy, deprived child who had hoped to find in Mr. Smith the father and mother *she* had missed. In addition to feeling deprived, hungry, and inept, Mrs. Smith was carrying a secret burden of shame: At the age of eight she had started a sexual relationship with a half brother that had lasted until she was about thirteen years old. As a consequence, she experienced herself not only as hungry and deprived, but also innately bad, corrupt, and sluttish.

Each, unable to give what the other expected, and frustrated with his (or her) own needs, increasingly tended to explode in front of the other. There were angry battles over who would prepare the breakfast or who would pay the bills. Sexual relations, which had been sporadic from the outset, stopped totally several years earlier when Mr. Smith became impotent. While their needs went unmet, they tried to manipulate each other by the use of physical symptoms and complaints and tried to dilute their rage as much as they could—by drinking, by withdrawing into sulky silences, by finding some niche (e.g., the father in his work, and the mother in social busybodiness) wherein each hoped to remain undisturbed by the other. To no avail: they remained centripetally deadlocked. Their rage, frustration, and depression mounted and they could not help turning to those persons who seemed God- (or devil-) sent to alleviate or resolve their misery—their children.

I shall restrict myself to describing what this implied for Cindy, and shall try to show how Cindy, by being subjected to her parents' mainly binding and delegating stratagems, was subjected to pressures which eventually threatened to bring about a schizophrenic breakdown.

THE BINDING, DELEGATING, AND
EXPULSION OF CINDY

In limiting myself to adducing one or two examples of the various modes and submodes outlined above, I shall begin with the mode of binding. Each parent, in varying degrees and ways, engaged Cindy in the binding mode on the three levels—the level of elementary satisfaction and dependency, the level of cognitive binding, and the exploitation of loyalty.

From the beginning, Mr. Smith set out to bind Cindy to himself by affording her a special, erotically tinged attention. When Cindy was a child, he played games with her which were overstimulating and sadomasochistic—e.g., by aggressively fondling her and even beating her; when she was an adolescent, he carried on these games in a more "sublimated" form. In a bittersweet, constantly escalating fashion he played with Cindy the game of "who could hurt whom most," that is, of who could get most deeply under the other's vulnerable skin. Erotic—or, if you wish, genital and pregenital—elements were visible to observers, but not to the participants themselves. For, in addition to, and interdigitating with, the binding via incestuous, sadomasochistic overstimulation, a binding via mystification, which I subsume under "cognitive binding," had taken hold of the protagonists. The father, far from noticing his sadomasochistic, erotic attraction to his daughter, had managed to misdefine and mislocate such attraction by defining their interaction in terms of Cindy's willful disobedience and his fatherly concern for her welfare. By and large, he succeeded in making Cindy accept this definition of their interpersonal reality. Cindy, in trying to make sense of her inner needs and experiences, therefore could not help starting on the wrong foot, as it were. In defining herself within the muddy cognitive framework which her father staked out, she remained bound to him. And, to the extent that she remained bound to him, her separation into the peer group was jeopardized.

The force of the third level of binding, through the exploitation of loyalty, was fully apparent only during the latter part of family therapy. By then, Cindy had made some progress in her individual sessions. She was beginning to push her individuation and separation, but felt an agonized concern over hurting her family should she dare to move out and become independent. She saw herself as hurting and betraying her family deeply and irreversibly and, in an effort to cope with her dilemma, she alternately tried to offer herself as redeemer and victim to her family. At one moment she tried to atone for her "breakaway wishes" by turning herself into a self-sacrificing family therapist; at other moments, particularly in those of depression and despair, she would depict her parents as either collapsing or ragefully retaliating in response to her centrifugal tendencies. Increasingly I came to see the glaring self-destructive features in Cindy's runaway episodes, such as letting herself be gang-banged and be "freaked out" on overdoses of LSD, as reflecting attempts to atone for her (largely unconscious) "breakaway guilt."

I omit examples of the mother's binding of Cindy, which were no less formidable than the father's, and turn to how Cindy was recruited as a delegate. (Again I restrict myself to mentioning only a few illustrative examples.)

First, Cindy, as her mother's ally, had to fulfill the mission of destroying the father—a mission which embroiled her in deep loyalty conflict.

In the Smith family neither parent could be considered clearly dominant. Each seemed to have an equal chance of winning over the children to his side. After a period of relatively frequent shifts in the children's loyalties, a line-up of "offspring allies" somewhat stabilized: the three older children had—albeit precariously—settled in the mother's, and the three younger ones in the father's camp. This line-up gave the mother an advantage in the strategic use of her "allies." For "her" children, being older, could run away (i.e., could be encouraged to run away) and thereby be used to agonize the father (by depriving him of quasi-incestuous pleasures and/or showing him up as a bad parent) while the three younger children, all of them still below the age of twelve, could not (yet) serve a similar purpose on behalf of the father. Not surprisingly, Mrs. Smith was gleeful when, during the family sessions and follow-up interviews, she reported on Cindy's runaway escapades while Mr. Smith listened in abject rage. His rage increased when it was revealed that Mrs. Smith, through telephone calls and third-party contacts, knew all along about Cindy's whereabouts during the runaway episodes while Mr. Smith was left in the dark.

In covertly encouraging her daughter's runaway ventures, however, Mrs. Smith—in her "unholy" alliance with Cindy—entrusted Cindy not only with the mission to antagonize the hated spouse, but she also burdened her with a more directly self-serving mission: to provide the mother with outside excitement (or id nutriment), which had become increasingly difficult to engender and obtain within the Smith family.

Frequently Mrs. Smith appeared greedily spellbound when Cindy gave hints of drug parties, illicit sex, and roadside adventurism. While feeding on Cindy's morbid exploits, she injected seemingly innocuous remarks or questions, which reflected her covert wish for heavier dosages of the same. Typically, while Cindy's administrator and therapist tried to nail down plans and structures which would contain Cindy's adventurism, she would ask her daughter, seemingly whimsically and innocently: "Isn't it time to run away again, Cindy?"

Yet—and this adds a further dimension to Cindy's conflicts of loyalties and missions—not only did Cindy seem to run away in response to covert proddings from her mother; she seemed to do so also in response to messages which came from her father. These messages, however, bespoke a different mission than seemed intended by her mother. Mrs. Smith encouraged Cindy to run away primarily because she needed Cindy to harass Mr. Smith and to provide her (and possibly the whole family) with id nutriment. Mr. Smith (himself deeply split in regard to what he wanted from Cindy), while trying to bind Cindy, seemed to need her also as an experimenter with that kind of free and unfettered life style which he himself was increasingly seeking—and fearing! Increasingly Mr. Smith revealed strong runaway tendencies of his own. These tendencies led him to actions which were peculiarly dissociated and halfhearted. For example, after talking a lot about moving to a particular midwestern city where he would start a new business, he finally visited that city to "nail down arrangements." But after he arrived in town, it turned out that no plans or preparations had been made. There was no one to see, no address to look up, no explorations to be made. Having nothing else to do, he visited a seafood restaurant and returned home. Toward the end of the family therapy, he put the house up for sale—more evidence of his runaway wishes. But, again, nothing came of this. While remaining halfheartedly and ambivalently stalemated in his own runaway longings, he appeared insatiable in wanting to know about Cindy's runaway exploits.

Finally, the parents entrusted Cindy with missions which, in the final analysis, served their own superegos. Both of them needed Cindy to realize various aspects of their own frustrated ego ideals—radiant beauty and glamour in the case of the mother, academic success in the case of the father. Each needed Cindy for the realization of what he or she felt most deeply and painfully lacking in him- or herself. The mother, an obese ugly duckling, tried to retrieve through Cindy the promise of physical beauty and attractiveness she herself despaired of realizing; the father, a high-school dropout, pushed Cindy to achieve an instant academic success he himself had failed to gain. Cindy tried hard again and again to fulfill her parents' unrealized ego ideals and, again and again, felt deeply conflicted and guilty for not being able to do so. (For how could she conceivably achieve bodily intactness and physical beauty as well as academic success when all her energies were drained by the task of reconciling many seemingly unsolvable delegated dilemmas?)

One such dilemma brings us to the second superego function of self-observation, which Cindy had to fulfill for her parents, i.e., the observation of the offspring by the parents as a substitute for the parents' own self-observation. Such substitute self-observation seems to play a crucial role in the development of the schizophrenic disturbance. As an example, the mother, instead of observing and coming to grips with her own sins and shame, recruited Cindy for this purpose. She had engaged in sexual relations with a half brother between the ages of eight and thirteen. This experience, never analyzed or worked through, came to envelop her in a pervasive sense of primitive, all-encompassing shame. In order to be able to deal with this shame, she needed (among other things) a sinful and shameful Cindy who would allow her to deal with her own sense of shame via projective identification. As it turned out, Cindy tried to comply with this covert need of her mother's by engaging in sinful and shameful acts.

Finally, Cindy gave us reason to believe that, in addition

to her other delegate functions, she had been fulfilling the mission of embodying her parents' primitive, punitive conscience. Much has been said about the cruel archaic conscience of schizophrenic patients. The more we get to know patients like Cindy and their families, the more we become aware that in this area also these patients are carrying burdens which they had to take over from others.

As of today, Cindy's future looks uncertain. When her therapist made plans to leave the area, Cindy ran away from the hospital. Even before this event, the family therapy had lagged. More than ever, the members had seemed stalemated in their hostility, had been absent, or had let the discussions become repetitive. Mr. Smith came closer and closer to expelling Cindy. He called her incorrigible, recalcitrant, a mischievous brat bent on her own and his destruction. But before he could expel her definitively, Cindy ran away.

After Cindy ran away, Mr. Smith tried to forget her. But as is typical in such cases, he could not; Cindy, although written off, remained to him an unending source of worry and guilty concern.

After several months on the road—spent mostly in the company of one runaway boyfriend—Cindy found a new family of sorts. This happened to be a religiously oriented commune with rather strict rules, located in a distant part of the country. So far, Cindy has abided by these rules and, in fact, has welcomed them. While settling down in her new "commune family," she has kept in touch with her mother. She writes her a letter once or twice a month and, in doing so, continues to serve as her mother's delegate. Held on the long leash of loyalty, she thus still serves as a pawn in her parents' battles, causing her father to fulminate at the thought that she "conspires" with her mother. Yet also, as she did earlier, Cindy unwittingly continues to serve the additional mission of providing both parents with vicarious thrills and runaway expertise.

Thus, although she is away from home, Cindy, the delegate, remains subject to conflicts of loyalty and missions. But for the moment she seems to have found a moratorium which alleviates these conflicts and she has gained a foothold in a world of peers and alternate adults that, problematic as it may appear, may promote her eventual liberation from her parents. Only time will tell whether and how such liberation will evolve.

8

Waywardness

In the preceding chapter, I outlined extremes of binding and delegating as seen in schizophrenia. Here I shall present a contrasting focus, intended to highlight extremes seen in the expelling mode—insidious parental neglect and rejection of children.

However, I must qualify the term "extremes." An early and total severence of the parent–child relationship precludes the child's survival, unless he finds a substitute parent or substitute home. We deal therefore with extremes in expulsion which accommodate some nonrejecting elements. These children have acquired a base for autonomous living despite—and partly because of—early and ongoing deprivation. This base allows them to survive their rejection and to turn into survival assets their (relative) lack of relatedness and lack of capacity for guilt and loyalty.

The term "wayward" reflects the epitome of the expelling mode. "Wayward," according to Webster's Dictionary, derives from "awayward," which means "turned away" and suggests expulsion as well as escape. The turned-away person is, again according to Webster's, self-willed, wanton, and prone to follow his or her own caprices. Along with that, he follows no clear principle or law and therefore does often the opposite of what is desired or expected. Such traits set the wayward person apart from the typical schizophrenic who, on closer inspection, appears constrained or smothered by laws and expectations deriving from others (covert and idiosyncratic as these might be).

Still, as commonly employed, the terms schizophrenia and waywardness may refer to similar or related phenomena because of the indiscriminate and—particularly in the case of schizophrenia—controversial use of the concepts (see Stierlin, 1967). Such overlap notwithstanding, the terms can cast into relief differing vicissitudes and dynamics of human relations.

Central here is the notion that the potentially schizophrenic person had one crucial experience which the potentially wayward person lacked—*the experience of having been important to at least one parent (or parent substitute)*. The young child, I have explained in my book, *Conflict and Reconciliation* (1969), needs to be loved and admired (i.e., to be found important), hopefully not because he or she "deserves" it, but simply because he or she is there, a little child. The potential schizophrenic, I submit, has been found important —although at an excessive price: his importance to his parents was made contingent on his remaining bound and delegated. But however heavy the price, he *was* found important.

This, I believe, is the main reason why he so frequently colludes in his enslavement and supplies the chains of guilt and loyalty which lock him and his parents into suffocating symbiosis. For where a sense of importance has been bestowed, hopes and cares have been kindled—hopes and cares which attach themselves even to an exploitative and squelching relationship. In contrast, in the potentially wayward child, such a sense of importance is lacking and there is therefore lacking that hope and caring investment in a relationship whose by-products are often excessive guilt and loyalty.

Here we may look at some of the late D. Winnicott's ideas on the positive aspects of guilt and loyalty. Guilt in particular, according to Winnicott (1958), implies a willingness and ability to take into account the other, and hence to register—although in an often distorted and exaggerated manner—the impact of one's aggression on him. There results, then, the need to "right" this aggression, for example, to deflect it from the other back onto the self or to atone for it through repair work. A certain amount of repair work, when integrated into an empathic and differentiated perception of the other, seems indispensible to individual growth. Winnicott cites the physician who, in treating his patients, embarks on a lifelong—and growth-producing—career of repair work.

At the root of such positive, growth-producing use of guilt and loyalty Winnicott sees a capacity called "concern." This capacity seems closely linked to how the child has been made to feel important. In the potential schizophrenic, this capacity for concern—and hence proneness to become bound through the chains of guilt and loyalty—seems perverted and exploited, but exists. In the potentially wayward child, by contrast, it appears weak and undeveloped. This, then, colors all of this child's quest for survival and affects, in particular, how he will separate in adolescence, the time when his libidinal and aggressive drives awaken, new cognitive skills emerge, and when ordinarily he must shift and modify his loyalties.

Let us, then, briefly consider two clinical syndromes which reveal features of waywardness, as here defined. I have in mind certain forms of narcissism and certain forms of sociopathy.

WAYWARDNESS AS NARCISSISM

H. Kohut (1966, 1971), above others, has explored and described narcissistic disturbances, and the following reflections draw on his insights. Kohut sees narcissistic disorders on a running scale that ranges from severe narcissistic neuroses to mild disturbances in self-esteem regulation. He thereby contradicts earlier psychoanalytic notions according to which libidinal development proceeds step-wise from narcissism to object love, while narcissistic involvement gradually diminishes and ultimately disappears. Kohut's conceptual framework allows for various forms and sources of narcissism. In the following, I shall focus on certain types of narcissistic individuals, mentioned by Kohut, and seen in my own practice, whom I came to view as "wayward."

These individuals are self-centered, but their egocentricity is not such as to let them lose touch with reality. Also, their personality organization is relatively stable and they differ therefore from so-called borderline patients who are more labile and whose hold on reality is precarious.

Being self-centered (or self-willed), such persons are unable to lastingly fall in love or be in love (despite and because of their often rampant promiscuity). In general, they seem so impervious to the presence and needs of others that these others hardly exist for them, unless they fulfill one crucial function, to be discussed shortly.

Also, like the wayward person in Webster's definition, they appear to follow their own caprices and—most important— seem not beholden to common values and principles. Their moral principles appear corruptible, in contrast, for example, to those of certain obsessive-compulsive patients who never find respite from their overconscientiousness. At the same time, these individuals seem free of the kind of guilt which agonizes more obsessive patients.

A number of such narcissistic individuals, and this accords further with Kohut's observations, seem unusually creative. This trait becomes somewhat understandable when we reason that creativity requires, first, a relative freedom from conventions (i.e., from ordinary regulatory expectations and principles) and that it reflects, second, an attempt at precocious psychic synthesis and autonomy. In creating his own world or vision, the narcissistic person "pushes"—frequently to the breaking point—his "self-willedness" and self-sufficiency.

This narcissistic person's most striking feature, though, is his seeming grandiosity, i.e., his excessive sense of self-importance. Such a sense of self-importance, however, reveals on closer inspection its very opposite, namely, a sensed *lack* of such importance and a desperate dread of being found insignificant, a dread which turns all his endeavors into one relentless quest for the confirmation of his (inwardly doubted) importance. His endless, and never resolvable, quest for importance causes him to recruit any person that comes along— in fact, any person who exists—as a potential admirer and hence confirmer of his importance. This provides the one significant exception to the narcissistic person's general imperviousness to others. These others count and are registered insofar as they bestow admiration and importance on him. This explains the seeming paradox that a person who strikes us as cold and indifferent to the needs and existence of others reacts with hurt and mortification to seemingly trivial or imagined slights from them. This overreactivity to real or assumed slights, according to Kohut, is perhaps the most important and problematical feature in these patients' transference relationships. Although they tend to treat their analyst as if he were air or a piece of disposable furniture (despite or because of their overt idealization of him), they are deeply hurt when the analyst seems to have forgotten some minute detail of their history or when he is a few minutes late—as this indicates to them that he does not consider them important.

Whence does such a narcissistic quest for self-importance arise? Here much needs to be better understood. It seems likely that there are different pathways to different types of narcissism and it is possible that the type under discussion has more than one pathway. Kohut's comments on some of these patients' early relationships with parents seem informative, though. When these parents are mentioned, they emerge as cold and depriving individuals. They seem to have failed to bestow on their would-be narcissistic children a solid sense of importance, i.e., a sense of being loved and admired in their own right. This accords with my own observations as a therapist of such patients. Whenever I got to know these patients in depth, I was impressed with how they seemed to have grown up in an interpersonal vacuum devoid of parental warmth, care, and concern. To be sure, their parents frequently had provided a stable home with material comforts and seemed neglecting rather than rejecting parents. Still, such neglect could not but have had an expelling effect and prevented these children from acquiring the capacity for concern which Winnicott described. In embarking on a lifelong, overcompensatory quest for importance, these children then tried to make assets out of their liabilities. Their egocentricity and relative freedom from common values and conventions, and hence from the bonds of loyalty and the pangs of guilt, seemed to help them to become precociously autonomous or even creative, and allowed them to recruit ever-new admirers to confirm their importance. Yet, even when successful, such endless seeking of importance seemed, at best, a respite. For a real sense of importance was elusive as long as they barred from their experience those very forces whose relative lack they had tried to exploit: concern, guilt, and loyalty.

WAYWARDNESS AS SOCIOPATHY

Like schizophrenia and narcissism, the term *sociopath* is over-inclusive and controversial. Still, it can be used to view another variety of wayward individuals who, like the above narcissistic persons, are largely in touch with reality and therefore appear nonpsychotic but who also differ from such narcissistic individuals.

These sociopathic persons can be called wayward because they, too, appear self-willed, indifferent to the needs of others, capricious, unprincipled, and not beholden to common laws and expectations. They, too, seem to lack a capacity for concern and the related capacities to experience guilt and loyalty. And their ego ideals often appear shallow and easily corrupted.

Their "turned-awayness" from others, however, is often not immediately apparent. For, unlike many seemingly aloof and self-contained narcissistic persons, such sociopathic individuals often seem "tuned" into their fellow man because of their ingratiating, seductive manner and skill. They can manipulate and "con" people, and feed on their needs. Here we find typically pimps and other operators who expertly exploit other people's needs for dependency, thrills, or self-aggrandisement.

Such skill at psychological manipulation serves them to outwit, subdue, or humiliate others. Basically, they see the human world as a jungle wherein *homo es homini lupus*. In order to survive in this jungle, they rely on manipulative skills or brute power and turn into survival assets their impaired capacities for concern and for the experience of guilt and loyalty.

Unlike the above narcissistic individuals, these sociopathic persons rarely seem creative, at least in a commonly accepted sense. For whatever creative potential they have seems channeled into the task of gaining power over others—by outwitting, manipulating, or oppressing them.

A further difference between narcissistic and sociopathic waywardness emerges: whereas the narcissistic person seeks importance by endlessly recruiting admirers, the sociopathic one seems to do so by dominating or humiliating others. Both activities suggest a craving for power. While the narcissist seems to crave power subtly, the sociopath does so often brutally and bluntly. Narcissistic and sociopathic cravings for power need not be mutually exclusive. We may think here of a person such as Reinhard Heydrich who was second in command after Himmler of Hitler's SS. The Czechs, in particular, suffered unspeakably under him and called him "the henchman." Heydrich appeared soft-spoken and almost effeminate, was always impeccably dressed, and loved Bach's music and Gothic cathedrals. Yet he was also so ruthless and power-hungry that even Himmler, against whom he eventually intrigued, came to dread him. (This fact, however, did not prevent Himmler from murdering thousands of innocent Czechs in reprisal for Heydrich's assassination at the hands of several Czech paratroopers.)

Ordinarily, though, narcissistic and sociopathic individuals seem to belong to different groups, despite their similar quests for importance. Even where the sociopath seems to seek admiration in fashions similar to the narcissistic person, his pursuit of such admiration seems to rely on the more flashy and conventional trappings of power such as expensive cars, female playmates, clothes, etc.

The sociopath's quest for importance, again, points to what he experienced—and often still experiences—at the hands of his expelling, i.e., neglecting or rejecting, parents. These parents frequently could not even provide a relatively stable home situation, as could many parents of narcissistic individuals. Hence these children lacked a needed early stabilization (as is more fully described in my book, *Conflict and Reconciliation*). Often they were treated inconsistently as well as brutally. This seems in accord with descriptions of life in the metropolitan ghetto from which many "successful" sociopaths emerge. Psychiatric authors such as S. Minuchin, et al. (1967), E. Pavenstadt (1965), H. Hendin (1969), and the autobiographical accounts of Claude Brown (1965) and Malcolm X (1965) depict a chaotic human scene wherein rejection, neglect, and brutality abound.

A "street kid" by the name of Ralph, makes this vivid when he writes:

From the first moment I was born my mother never caged me in. I learned everything about the streets while growing up. When I was about 7 I got my first fuck. It was a small peanut but the girl didn't mind. I learned the good and the bad—not from my mother but from all my mothers, brothers and sisters in El Barrio. I seen shoot-outs with blacks and cops and gangs killing each other. Bullets going through my window. I learned everything I had to learn to survive in the streets. . . . (L. Cole, 1970)

All this seems in accord with my previously stated view that only the "strongest" expellees can make it as successful sociopaths. For only these youngsters, it seems, succeed in turning their liabilities (i.e., their impaired capacity for concern, guilt, and loyalty) into survival assets. Many others, who are less tough, seem to go under. They become frightened, demoralized, human driftwood; wayward youth with varying pictures of psychic arrest and disorganization, often suggesting a diagnosis of amorphous schizophrenia rather than that of sociopathy.

THE WAYWARD EXPELLEE IN
THE RUNAWAY CULTURE

Wayward expellees, we saw, often turn into casual runaways. Let us, then, briefly consider how the modern runaway culture mirrors the input of these wayward expellees with their particular problems, needs, and skills.

This runaway culture, we must remember, is complex and changing. It is shaped by the needs and contributions of the approximately six hundred thousand young persons who run away from their homes each year, and it is as diverse and pluralistic as the modern American society of which it forms a part. Within this large runaway culture, the wayward expellees—many, if not most of them casual runaways—form only one segment. This segment, however, is important and seems to account for some striking features of this subculture.

These features are the antithesis of the "loving togetherness," as originally reflected in the "Spirit of Woodstock" and *The Greening of America* (C. Reich, 1970), with their visions of intimate communal living freed of aggression and power ploys. Such visions blurred as time went by and more detailed and objective studies of the runaway subculture accumulated. These studies, provided by such sympathic observers as L. Ambrosino (1971) and B. Wein (1970), contradicted notions of the runaways' joyful and liberated togetherness and, instead, depicted a grim struggle for survival. This struggle for survival—taking shape in crash pads, metropolitan hangouts, and dope cellars—casts into relief the particular strengths, needs, and problems of wayward expellees. It also provides the background against which some ideological assertions of this culture's adolescents need to be seen.

One such assertion concerns the devaluation of lasting commitments of any sort. The late F. Perls, for one, became a spokesman for this ideological stance. In one of his best-known quotes, inscribed on the counterculture's perhaps most popular poster (depicting a loving, youthful couple surrounded by beautiful nature), he denounces the need to live up to the other's expectations. Instead, he extolls the "beautiful" chance encounter that is free of fetters. Thus, he de-emphasizes loyalty and dispells any guilt about failing and breaking away from this other.

Another such assertion, related to the above, concerns everybody's right "to do one's own thing." This widely held ideologic assertion can almost be called the counterculture's moral credo. At closer inspection, it appears a new version of the "rugged American individualism" of earlier days, its ruggedness now cloaked and blunted by the gentle rhetoric of loving togetherness. Like this earlier individualism, the "doing of one's own thing" overemphasizes the individual's right to self-actualization as against the willingness to show solidarity with, and to make sacrifices for, others.

It is in the runaway's daily struggle for survival that these two ideological postures—the advocacy of noncommitment and that of "doing your own thing"—reveal some of their implications. Noncommitment becomes here congruent with a nomadic way of life which requires the frequent change of one's abode, friends, and sex mates. But though congruent with life on the road, it does not necessarily foster or imply growth as we have come to understand it.

The "doing of your own thing," likewise, loses some of its luster when examined in the light of the runaway's actual life.

For "doing your own thing" here often entails that "the other's thing" is hurt, as when one's pushing of illicit drugs implies that new customers—i.e., as yet unsuspecting young adolescents—will be hooked.

If these reflections are correct, the runaway culture should also reveal an excessive quest for self-importance on the part of many of its members. This expectation, too, seems borne out by what we observe. Notwithstanding their advocacy of a simple, authentic, and noncompetitive life—as movingly depicted in C. Reich's *The Greening of America* (1970)— many of these counterculture members seem desperately driven to stand out and catch the limelight, although often via values and behavior that seem antithetical to what bestows prestige and importance in the "straight" culture. Hence, many youngsters seem driven to appear more dirty, have longer hair, and be more jarringly obscene than their peers. They may even proudly show their needle marks or boast of their many freakouts in order to gain importance. The competition that reigns in the denounced conventional world seems here merely transposed. As in the "conventional" world, we find a "dramaturgy of appearances" or "impression management" of the kind which E. Goffmann (1959, 1967) has described. This is a life style wherein "loyalty, security, gratitude, love and friendship are seen as forces of maudlin sentimentality."

Finally, we are not surprised to find—again in antithesis to the counterculture's manifest advocacy of "love," sincerity, and togetherness—a frequent glorification of power and violence. Brute power, we saw, is the wayward sociopath's main vehicle for finding importance. In retrospect, therefore, it was almost inevitable that Woodstock—originally hailed as a "watershed" in the emergence of a new man and culture— would be followed by Altamont where on December 6, 1969,

161

the Hell's Angels, surrounded and silently supported by a crowd of fascinated onlookers, clubbed and stabbed to death a young black man.* And it seems no wonder that the Hell's Angels and their like, in flaunting their steel helmets, swastikas, and motorcycles, seem to have caught the attention of youthful movie audiences more strongly than their more peaceful and self-effacing counterparts.

PARENTS OF WAYWARD EXPELLEES

Who are the parents of wayward expellees? What causes these parents to insidiously neglect and reject their children and to push them into premature autonomy? At this point, I shall not explore these questions in depth. Instead, I want to offer some thoughts and observations which derive from the above conceptual and clinical perspectives.

These parents, no less than those of predominantly bound and delegated children, seem caught up in a middle-age crisis. Often they seek a centrifugal solution to it; they want to make new starts, search for satisfactions and security outside the family orbit, but, in so doing, experience their children as hindrances.

An attempted centrifugal crisis solution, though, seems often colored and thwarted by one overriding fact, affecting particularly poor and/or black parents—a relentless struggle for survival.

Betty Jackson, portrayed in a special *Time* magazine issue on American women of March 20, 1972, provides an example.

---

* See the report by Nicholas von Hoffmann, "Violence at Altamont," *The Washington Post*, Friday, January 2, 1970.

She may or may not be a parent of wayward expellees, but reflects the struggle for survival many such parents face.

At age fifteen, we learn, Betty had an illegitimate child and that, coupled with the death of her mother, was "the end of my hopes." Migrating to New York City in 1960, she worked for four years as a live-in maid until another pregnancy caused her to lose her job. She has been on welfare since.

Presently living in a four-room ghetto apartment in the Bronx with four of her seven illegitimate children, Betty Jackson says, "I live in dope city and on one of the worst streets. The apartment has been robbed three times, and I've been cut once. We have no heat. We get hot water once in a while. The wall is coming apart from the leaks. I've had a broken window for the past year. The kids sleep in their clothes. I use a stove and oil for heat, but the gas and electricity bills are very high. I had an electric heater once, but it was stolen. Roaches are everywhere. The rats minuet and waltz around the floor."

While welfare pays her monthly rent of $92.10, she says that the additional $128 she receives twice a month barely allows for the necessities. "I am a slave to my financial problems," she says, "and my life is meaningless as far as having things that people are supposed to have." Now thirty-six, she says of the three men who sired her children that "I have never come close to getting married." Though she has had a tubal ligation to prevent further pregnancies, the pattern remains. She says that whatever hopes she had of returning to work were dashed when her nineteen-year-old daughter gave birth to an illegitimate child two weeks earlier. Survival, she explains, is her primary concern.

When asked about the future, she answered, "If things don't shape up, my children won't live for it. Society will kill them and put them in bondage too, and they won't be able to move either." Summing up her plight, Betty Jackson says, "I just need some place to survive. I am being crazied up by this Establishment."

In Betty Jackson's case, it seems mainly the struggle for *material* survival that contributes to her failure as an executive, caring parent. Most expelling parents of the white middle class have no comparable material worries, although their jobs and finances, too, may be in disarray. Theirs is a different struggle with psychological rather than material poverty. When trying to cope with such psychological poverty, these parents seem unable to bind or delegate people (and particularly their children) to any significant degree, as they must relentlessly seek importance. Thus, they bypass their children or see them as threats and nuisances.

Essentially, parents can pursue the quest for importance via two frequently overlapping routes: the *narcissistic* route of achieving artistic, scholastic, or managerial success, or the more *sociopathic* route of seeking exploitative power. (Typically, the greater the power enjoyed and achieved, the more difficult it is to apply to these people the label of sociopath at least during their lifetimes, as it is usually only the downtrodden and expendable people for whom we reserve demeaning and incriminatory labels.)

In many expelling parents, we discover the (often covert and disguised) traits of wayward expellees, albeit these appear often justified. We hear of these parents' unusual devotion to their work, their putting in an eighteen-hour day seven days a week, their "creative drivenness," their service for the common good. Whatever the justifications, many of them neglect their children while they belatedly seek importance.* They do so because they were not found suffi-

---

* Of course, parents may seek importance also as *their* parents' unwitting delegates.

ciently important when it counted most, when they were growing children. While not considered important, they had to make the best of their push into premature autonomy. Having grown into parents themselves, they cannot but expel —i.e., insidiously neglect or reject—their own children in turn. Seen from this perspective, these parents, too, like the massively binding parents discussed in the foregoing, remain beholden to their interpersonal past, while they make their children the graves of their hopes and needs.

9

The Liberation of
Middle-Aged Parents

Here I want to sketch out a general perspective which bears on the therapy of parents *and* adolescent children. Central to this perspective is the concept of *liberation*. It evokes a picture of shackles thrown away, of resurging life and hope, of release from oppressive and exploitative environments, and from oppressive and exploitative others.

Liberation, thus understood, is an individual and transactional phenomenon. It is an individual phenomenon because joy, a sense of relief, and upsurging energies and hopes are individually experienced. It is a transactional phenomenon because the oppressive environment and oppressive others must change along with the oppressed individual in order for liberation to occur. Optimally, such liberation is therefore *mutual*. Oppressor and oppressed, jailer and prisoner, enslaver and slave, exploiter and exploited, each gains a new freedom. This, then, indicates as well as propels an expanding interpersonal dialectic or positive mutuality.

The parent who wants to master his or her crisis of middle age must, I believe, aim at such mutual liberation, i.e., a liberation that frees not only oneself, but also one's—real or presumed—oppressor or exploiter. From the vantage point of this study, it is most frequently one's spouse or adolescent children whom this parent, overtly or covertly, casts into an oppressor or exploiter role, just as the latter feels opppressed and exploited by him or her. What, then, does such liberation, aiming at mutuality, require from the middle-aged parent?

In a most general sense, it requires that he or she, in characteristic ways, reconcile what I have elsewhere (1969)— following J. Baldwin (1895, 1899, 1915) and E. Becker (1962, 1964)—described as the basic tasks of doing and undergoing. Through *doing*, one asserts one's interests, shows initiative, stakes out one's goals, needs, and priorities. One asserts one-self as a center of executive, self-responsible action. Such doing implies *owning*—an owning not only of one's needs, intentions, and fantasies, but also of one's conflicts, one's ambivalences, one's dark sides, one's deficiencies, one's failures for which one assumes responsibility. Owning, thus understood, means pain of the kind which accompanies true growth.

Undergoing implies an ability and willingness to be affected by the other and to be receptive to his or her needs, wishes, and growth—even when this other is experienced as oppressor or exploiter.

In such reconciliation of doing and undergoing, liberation becomes mutual, in contrast to the one-sided pseudoliberation of the revolutionary who, in his moment of triumph, turns into vengeful counteroppressor and thereby perpetuates a negative mutuality; rather, a positive mutuality through which both parties gain a new awareness of, and freedom for, each other, is needed.

When we examine the liberation of middle-aged parents with this model in mind, we can again take the concept of transactional modes as our guide. We can then distinguish between different tasks and pathways of liberation which reflect several levels of the needed reconciliation of doing and undergoing.

PARENTS' LIBERATION THROUGH THEIR WORK ON THEIR RELATIONSHIP WITH THEIR PARENTS

On a first level, we deal with these parents' liberation from their own parents—either internalized or living parents. "Liberation work" on this first level affects how these parents may liberate themselves from their spouses and children. Such first-level liberation work will then differ depending on whether these parents, as children of their own parents, were —or still are—predominantly bound, delegated, or expelled, according to these assumptions:

1. *Predominantly binding parents* were—and often still are—bound by their own parents.

2. *Predominantly delegating parents* were—and often still are—delegated by their own parents.

3. *Predominantly expelling parents* were—and often still are—expelled by their own parents.

In brief: as a result of having themselves been bound, delegated, or expelled, these parents' liberation from their own parents remained aborted. They became burdened with the task of living with, and having to undo, the consequences of their own boundness, delegation, or expulsion. This, then, caused them to interfere with the kind of mutual liberation that could free their spouses and children, and themselves as well. Liberation work on this level requires a parent to come to grips with what his or her own parents did to him or her.

168

It implies the owning and working through of the fury, rage, and disappointment about what one's parents failed to be and about what they have done to their child, now turned parent. Hopefully, this work can result in mourning, resignation, and forgiveness, allowing not only personal growth but also a new awareness and acceptance of one's own parents with all their weaknesses and strengths.

Where one's parents have died, such liberation work, inevitably, remains limited to memories and those internalized offshoots from these parents—such as unquestioned identifications, values, and expectations (held for oneself as well as for one's spouse and children)—which now powerfully shape one's life. Where these parents are still alive, the liberation work can involve them as active participants. This happens now more frequently through family therapy, as the transactional literature shows. Particularly I. Boszormenyi-Nagy (1965a, 1966, 1972) has come to advocate a three-generational approach, but also S. Fisher (1956) and D. Mendell (1956, 1958), and M. Bowen (1965, 1966), for example, have reported on family therapies that involved three generations. In these therapies, the middle-aged parents worked face to face with their own parents and their liberation from them could be directly fostered as well as studied.

Such a three-generational setting provides perhaps the strongest evidence for the correctness of the above working assumptions—at least as far as predominantly binding and delegating parents of parents are concerned. (Markedly expelling parents of parents are unlikely participants in such three-generational therapy and hence less easy to study.) We are now apt to observe how the mother who binds her adolescent child is still bound by her own mother. We notice, for example, how the mother who mystifies and regressively gratifies her teenaged daughter is still held captive to her own mother who, a frequent visitor to her house, showers her with gifts and gives her confusing messages as to what she should, and should not, do. Or, we observe directly how a father who delegates his son of average intellectual gifts to become an outstanding academic success still reels under his own father's expectations—now proven to be outlandish and unfulfillable —to become a famous professor.

Much liberation work on this first level, though, must occur in the absence of the parents' parents, as these are either unavailable or dead. The parents' liberation must now proceed through what transpires in individual, family, or couple therapy or, where this is not feasible, through the ordinary vicissitudes of human relations. The parents' parents, and the parents' relations to them, come alive through memories and associations which the therapeutic process activates. These memories and associations become more charged with emotions the more the therapy turns "three dimensional," that is, the more it links the transactional present to the transactional past.

Such liberation from one's own parents—be these one's internalized or living parents—implies a reconciliation of doing and undergoing: it implies a new assertion vis-à-vis these parents, a new staking out of one's needs, goals, and priorities in relative freedom from what these parents expected, or still expect, for oneself. And this implies an "owning" of one's obligations (difficult as these may be to measure), of one's failures and deficiencies, as well as of one's conflicts and ambivalences, even though these can be rightly attributed to one's parents. Especially conflicts over individuation and conflicts of loyalties and missions, as described in Chapters 4 through 7, need to be owned, i.e., felt and grappled with in one's insides. Undergoing, on the other hand, implies that one can, despite and because of one's self-assertions, remain affected by, and related to, one's parents; that in the final analysis one can accept what one became through them and what they did to oneself.

Grief, mourning, and resignation mark this liberation from one's own parents. For various losses must be endured and accepted such as, for example, the loss of the idealized image of one's parents (which served to hide and disown the underlying rage and disappointment felt toward them) or, on the opposite pole, the loss of a convenient target for one's projections and vilifications.

Such mourning can occur in relatively undramatic and inconspicuous ways, reflecting as well as triggering a new empathic seriousness apparent in the family, couple, or individual therapy, as well as in one's outside relations. Or it can occur dramatically—experienced in acute, piercing grief— and then can have an immediate liberating impact, as N. Paul and G. Grosser (1965), among others, have shown.

LIBERATION THROUGH WORK ON
THE MARITAL RELATIONSHIP

Liberation on this second level—which concerns one's spouse and marriage—interweaves with that occurring on the first level. On this second level, too, liberation must become three-dimensional, that is, must link the transactional present to the transactional past.

In line with our conceptual model, mutual liberation can here fail in contrasting ways: it can fail when the spouses remain centripetally deadlocked, when they continue to chafe under a squelching pseudomutuality or pseudohostility. And it can fail when they succumb too easily to centrifugal pulls. For then they run the danger of separating from each other before they have really met.

Depending on whether they are married in a predominantly centripetal or centrifugal pattern, middle-aged spouses face different problems of liberation. The concept of liberation, in its strictest meaning, applies only to centripetal deadlocks. If it is to apply also to centrifugal situations, we must qualify it. Let us, then, consider briefly how liberation from a centripetal deadlock may show up in couple or family therapy.

Such a deadlock, according to my experience, often loosens once a three-dimensional (or multigenerational) outlook emerges. Typically, the parents begin to realize that they subjected, and are subjecting, each other to conflicting expectations. For example, a wife realizes that she wants her husband to be weak and subservient as her own father was but, at the same time, wants him to be her "self-assertive delegate" (note the contradiction of terms) who vicariously fulfills her wishes for competitive masculine conquest. The husband, in turn, realizes that he wants his wife to be an adoring, self-effacing housekeeper and mother, to serve as a glamorous advertisement for his social success, and, at the same time, wants her to embody regenerative maternal strength and nurturance—to be given unstintingly to him, the husband child. Particularly R. Laing, et al. (1966) and, more recently, C. Sager, et al. (1971) have described such incompatible perceptions and expectations of spouses. These expectations reveal the binding and delegating impact of these spouses' own parents. Where a three-dimensionality develops, the spouses can correct and reorganize their perceptual and experiential field and thus can loosen the centripetal deadlock. In the process, many of these parent-spouses terminate what M. Bowen (1965) has called their "emotional divorce"; they experience a new, and often first, honeymoon, discovering now ever-new sides in each other. We see a positive mutuality unfold before our eyes.

In contrast, many centrifugally oriented (and not seldom narcissistic) parents must first discover that they are, or can be, significant to each other before they can experience true liberation. They must, first of all, allow themselves to be tamed—i.e., have their importance confirmed through an intimate, enduring relationship—as did the fox in Saint-Exupéry's story of *The Little Prince*. And, as therapists of these frequently narcissistic patients and parents can attest, their chances for such "taming" are often not good. Yet only after they are tamed, that is, have established firm and mutual bonds of loyalty and concern, can they hope to liberate themselves from each other in the above stricter meaning of the term.

PARENTS' LIBERATION THROUGH THEIR WORK ON THEIR RELATIONSHIP WITH THEIR ADOLESCENT CHILDREN

Here we deal with a third level of needed "liberation" work. In negotiating their separation from their adolescent children, many parents get their last chance to loosen the shackles which tie them to *their* parents. Where they miss such a chance, the adolescent, rather than triggering their liberation, becomes the grave of their hopes, as I have indicated in Chapters 7 and 8. In the interest of parents *and* their adolescent children, liberation must become mutual.

Here we must again adopt a three-dimensional (or three-generational) perspective. We see, then, how parents lead their adolescent children along the same routes that their own parents led them, and how they use their children for overdue repair work, caused by their own parents. At the same time, we notice how these parents exploit their children for the purpose of making viable a nonviable marriage. I. Boszormenyi-Nagy and G. Spark (1973) have thoroughly elaborated this perspective.

Parents and adolescent children must also here reconcile doing and undergoing. In doing, parents assert their interests and convictions, take responsibility for their actions and obligations, "own" their failures and deficiencies, and, most important, own the conflicts and ambivalences that mark their middle-age crisis, which they so far disowned by binding or delegating their children. In undergoing, parents open themselves to their children's true needs, interests, and messages, and thereby use the opportunity offered them by the latter to gain new freedom and leverage for resolving their crisis of middle age.

The specifics of such mutual liberation must again vary, depending on which transactional mode prevails.

Where the binding mode is dominant, it is the adolescent's striving to "unbind" himself or herself—hidden and complicated as such striving may be—which offers parents their truest hope for their own liberation. Any attempt by an adolescent to unbind himself cannot but upset his binding parents and, for a while, deepen their anxieties and crisis. However, this adolescent fulfills a function for his parents similar to that which the heretic and "separatist" Martin Luther fulfilled for the Catholic church in the sixteenth century. Without Luther's action, that church very likely would have disintegrated under the weight of its sticky, unchecked corruption. By challenging the corruption, Luther forced the church to reform itself, while he, in separating himself from it, bore the onus of rebel and heretic.

174

In unbinding himself or herself, the adolescent can help the parents to get in touch with what their own parents did to them. A therapist who is objective as well as empathically close to the transacting parties can aid this process. For example, a binding mother who berates her adolescent daughter for "willfully and selfishly" seeking friends instead of considering her loving mother, suddenly remembers in a joint session how she herself, as an adolescent, suffered similar binding stratagems from her own mother. The liberating effect of such a shift in a parent's perspective—away from the adolescent and to one's own parents—can be immediate as well as lasting. The mother now experiences sadness, pangs of guilt, but also relief. Over time, these emotions create a new attitude toward her child which is more differentiated, more reflective, and more empathic than the one she mustered before. The same happens to the child in relation to her.

Similar considerations apply to predominantly delegating parents. Adolescents who refuse to be delegated, and hence try to escape the conflicts of loyalty and mission, also promote their parents' liberation. They cause these parents to own or reown their so-far disowned ambivalences and conflicts and thereby force them to struggle with their marital deadlock and with what their parents did to them.

Where we find predominantly expelling parents and neglected children, the meaning of mutual liberation must again be qualified. In order to liberate himself in the above meaning of the term, the expelled adolescent needs, first of all, to be found important by his own parents. Therefore he needs to challenge these parents, engrossed in their importance seeking, to stop neglecting him. By rebelling against his expulsion and by insisting on *his* importance, this adolescent, too, helps his parents with their overdue repair work. Possibly he forces them now to realize how they were found unimportant by their own parents and hence were pressured into their (interpersonally disastrous) importance seeking.

The liberation of expelled and neglected adolescents appears analogous to that of many expelled and neglected poor people. These poor, too, seem destined to pass their lives in the darkness of unimportance of which B. Brecht (1967) has written. Many rich—i.e., "important"—members of the society are indifferent to their sufferings and treat them as expendable human surplus. In order to liberate themselves from the rich, the poor must therefore first establish their importance—to themselves and to the rich. As part of such an attempt, they may need to attack the rich and, in so doing, depict the rich as actively exploitative oppressors, while the rich are, in fact, "merely" indifferent. By hating the rich—and inviting hate in return—the poor hope to establish a relationship that, paradoxically, can be more humane and psychologically easier to endure than a nonrelationship caused by the rich people's indifference. Being hated and attacked implies now that one is somebody and is important. The poor thus not only mitigate the pain of having their pain ignored, they also prepare the ground for an eventual mutual liberation in the above meaning of the term.

THE PARENTS' LIBERATION IN MODERN SOCIETY

We are now in a position to take a new look at the liberation of middle-aged parents within our modern American society. This society is pluralistic, mobile, and subject to accelerating change. Relentlessly it seems to push toward a new democratic and equalitarian consciousness wherein new rights and life styles—such as those of women, blacks, children—are asserted and frequently, albeit reluctantly and belatedly, conceded.

From the vantage point of middle-aged parents bent on their liberation, this society appears in a dual light. (Primarily, I think here of middle-class parents who, unlike the poor and black Betty Jackson, described in Chapter 8, are not overwhelmed by a relentless struggle for material survival.) More than ever before, society offers them new opportunities for self-realization, new starts and careers, new marriages, or for new and unconventional types of relationships. But such new opportunities, and this reflects the other side of the coin, also imply new opportunities for conflict and failure. In moving more actively into this society, these parents inevitably expose themselves to competition, to loneliness, to overstimulation, and to the realization that what they learned or did in the past ill equips them for new starts. In brief, they must have a new strength and capacity to own and to take responsibility for their actions, deficiencies, and conflicts, in order that they can realize the promise of liberation.

Middle-aged parents need such strength in order that they can make it in the new runaway culture for adults. Where such strength is lacking, "runaway parents" risk a rude awakening. Their situation differs little from that of their runaway children who, instead of realizing new opportunities and freedom, become stranded in lonely, crime-ridden human wastelands.

The construct of transactional modes alerts us here to a paradox. For it appears that predominantly binding and delegating parents (who, as we saw, have become bound themselves by their spouses and parents) could best utilize such new opportunities, i.e., they could become "dropout wives or husbands" or start new careers. In making such new starts, they could break their centripetal deadlock and gain the breathing space needed to make their liberation three-dimensional and mutual. But centrifugal, liberating moves, we find on closer inspection, seem impossible or unthinkable for many of these parents. Geared to bind and delegate others, and to be bound and delegated in turn, these parents are apt to see only the dangers, and not the opportunities, involved in liberating moves. They dread the loneliness, failure, and defeat they believe to be in store for them should they move into the cold, bewildering, competitive world; and it might take time and therapy before they can take advantage of society's opportunities, i.e., can dare to make new starts and—in so doing—can risk loneliness and defeat. This, paradoxically, will probably not result in the dreaded breakup of their marriage or family but will rather reshuffle the existing balance in interpersonal closeness and distance so as to promote a mutual liberation.

But what looks like an opportunity from the vantage point of predominantly binding and delegating parents can look differently from that of predominantly expelling parents. By submitting easily to society's centrifugal pull, these parents cannot but fail in their liberation. They yield merely to the temptation of seeking importance, by way of anonymous admiration or by way of brute power, at the expense of relationship work at home that is as urgent as it is overdue. A patient of mine, brilliant as a lawyer and prominent as a politician, is an example. Married and divorced three times, and the father of three children, he never saw these children, as he relentlessly craved work sixteen hours a day. He related to his girlfriends in different cities—which he visited under the requirements of his job—in a fleeting, uncommitted way. His history revealed an alcoholic father and a neglectful, depressed, and emotionally unavailable mother who made him seek his salvation through early independence, power, and glamour. There was evidence that underneath his hectic search for importance he experienced guilt and despair about neglecting and expelling his children as he himself had been neglected and expelled. But this issue could not be worked through because his search for importance and power interfered with a therapy that would have required his long-term investment.

10

The So-Called
Conflict of Generations

Traditionally, the separation drama in adolescence has been
cast as a "conflict of generations." In these summarizing remarks, I want to reflect on what such a conflict of generations may mean in the light of the model I presented.

The term "conflict," in order to become meaningful, presupposes parties whose vital needs and interests clash. Hence,
they have to assert these needs and interests by overtly or
covertly fighting each other. Let us, then, briefly consider how
the two parties in the so-called conflict of generations—adolescents and parents—define and assert vis-à-vis each other
their vital needs and interests.

For adolescents, these needs and interests seem shaped by
the three main features mentioned earlier: the intensification
of their drives, their cognitive maturation, and their (relative)
transfer of loyalties—*away from* their parents *to* peers and
alternate adults of their choosing. These three features, above
others, account for the momentum of adolescence. As such,
they are apt to shift the balance of power between the generations. Their vitality heightened, adolescents can, more force-

fully and articulately than before, assert their needs and priorities, can unmask their exploiting or expelling parents, and can turn away from the latter.

The parents, their vitality declining, are vulnerable to such assertion, yet can muster resources of their own. They can use their economic power, influence, and superior knowledge (particularly of the adolescent's weakness) to fight or manipulate him successfully.

The question is now: Can mutual liberation occur in the context of this conflict of generations? My answer is yes—when the conflict remains or becomes a "loving fight" (see Levi, Stierlin, Savard, 1972) wherein the parties, instead of trying to devastate each other, affirm each other's right to exist.

In order for this to happen, the following are required.

First, the two parties must strive to differentiate and to articulate their differing needs and interests. From a position of "articulate separateness," they must be able and willing to share a common focus of attention and ensure an ongoing communication and relatedness. Such ongoing communication on the basis of articulate separateness differs from the blurry, sticky boundness found in families with schizophrenic offspring, but it also differs from the alienation and breakdown of communication found in many expelling, centrifugal relationships.

A loving fight implies, second, a deepening awareness of the parties' interdependence and mutual obligations. Such awareness can counteract each party's pursuit of self-interest and power. It balances self-assertive "doing" with other-oriented "undergoing."

Third, a loving fight, in reconciling doing and undergoing for each party, promotes each party's repair work, as outlined in Chapter 9. It allows for a three-dimensionality of liberation that, ideally, can include the parents' parents and the children's as yet unborn children.

The conflict of generations, instead of becoming a loving fight, can either remain aborted or turn into a fight to the death in which both parties must lose. The concept of transactional modes permits us to sketch out several negative outcomes of intergenerational conflict.

Where extreme binding prevails, the conflict of generations remains aborted and hence cannot develop into a loving fight. For severe binding interferes with the differentiation and articulation of separate needs and positions. Therefore, mutual growth and repair work are impeded. In extreme cases, the child is condemned to live out a shadow death, while his parents are crushed by, and yet cannot mourn, the loss of the hopes and desires they invested in their child.

Where expelling prevails, a precociously articulate separateness can be achieved at the price of arrested growth and a lacking sense of importance. Yet without a sense of importance, mutually bestowed, a loving fight cannot develop.

Where adolescents are predominantly delegated, the conflict of generations often seems blatant and intense. Here we find many—perhaps most—adolescents who flaunt their rebellion by taking drugs, who defy authorities and conventions, are sexually promiscuous, and run away. Typically, in family therapy these youths are labeled as the most "rebellious" and defiant of all siblings. Such labeling, though, is misleading, as most of these adolescents, far from being the most rebellious, turn out to be the most loyal and compliant children. Their rebelliousness is spurious because they do only what their parents wish them to do. In taking drugs, engaging in promiscuous sex, or defying conventions, they respond—albeit in often fumbling and seemingly contradictory ways—to their parents' covert expectations. Where they are torn by conflicts, these are chiefly conflicts of loyalties and conflicts of missions with which their parents burdened them. Although their prospects for growth and separation are better than those of massively bound and expelled adolescents, these youngsters, too, miss out on an articulate separateness that could sustain a loving, liberating fight.

A FINAL NOTE ON RUNNING AWAY

In this book, I have reflected on runaway adolescents, runaway parents, and the modern runaway culture. Now that I come to the end, the final analysis reveals that running away has little chance to succeed. By running away, we can establish temporary distance, yes. We can find temporary relief, yes. We can find new opportunities and make new starts, yes. We can even experience a resurgence of life and hope. But at one point we must stop running and take stock. When we do so, we find the other, be he or she parent or child, around us and in ourselves—and this other never stops challenging us to engage with him or her in a loving fight that aims at a mutual, three-dimensional liberation.

11

On the Family Therapy of Adolescents

Since the first edition of *Separating Parents and Adolescents*, I have, with the help of members of our Heidelberg team, developed further the interactional model presented in the original edition. Today it takes the form of an integrative model that relates to other research as well as to our own contributions and ideas. At present it comprises five (sometimes overlapping) main perspectives, each of which comprehends central systemic forces and indicates the direction of therapy. Against the background of the original concepts first discussed in this book in 1974, it is necessary to outline the central elements of the current model.

The five perspectives may be compared with the lens of a telescope: They bring certain aspects of the observational field into sharp focus but obscure others or leave them in a marginal blur. At the same time, the perspectives provide a therapeutic frame of reference. It is above all this framework and its relevance to the therapy of adolescents undergoing separation that concerns us in this final chapter of the new edition of *Separating Parents and Adolescents*.

184

THE FIRST MAIN PERSPECTIVE: RELATED
INDIVIDUATION

The concept of individuation implies primarily the development and maintenance of individual characteristics and phychological boundaries. Such individuation makes it possible for us to experience ourselves in the most diverse interpersonal contexts as separate but at the same time related. It means the differentiation of the inner personality into conscious and unconscious spheres; clear, articulate feelings, needs, and expectations; inner and outer perceptions; and the demarcation of a differentiated inner world from the outer world, in particular from the ideas, needs, expectations, and demands of others. Individuation is always important and is at the same time tested when emotional closeness and empathy characterize a human relationship. It is both the precondition and expression of successful separation and reconciliation in adolescence.

The concept of *related individuation* describes both the behavior of individuals—for example, an adolescent in a one-to-one relationship—or that of several people—for example, members within a family. Disturbances of related individuation are present when members are insufficiently differentiated from one another, are merged symbiotically with one another, or are isolated in a rigid and noncommunicating stance. Each individual case involves either underindividuation or overindividuation.

Disorders of related individuation are involved in the derailment of the relational modes I have described as *binding, delegating,* and *expelling.* Nevertheless, related individuation— its dynamic and disturbances—forms an aspect distinct from these relational modes.

In the drama of separation in adolescence, psychoanalytic authors have until now primarily stressed the significance of individuation as the capacity to differentiate personal feelings, expectations, positions, etc. The concept of related individuation means that separation alone is not enough; it must be accompanied by relatedness and embedded in a continuing relationship.

Both differentiation from and relatedness to others are revealed most meaningfully in the capacity and willingness to take part in a dialogue. In a dialogue, different feelings, expectations, and positions are expressed; a common focus is shared; conflicts are defined; and mutual affirmation and recognition are accorded. At its fullest development, a dialogue becomes what I have designated *positive mutuality* (1971, p. 60). Typically, adolescent runaways avoid such dialogue. They differentiate themselves by running away and either will not or can no longer talk to their parents. The aim of therapy is therefore to establish or reestablish the possibility of dialogue between the generations.

Some Therapeutic Consequences of These Perspectives

"Establishing the possibility for dialogue" means principally:

1. *Training in communicative dialogue.* This includes training in the use of the first-person singular (for example, "*I* feel like this"; "*I* expect this"; "*I* hope that" instead of "one" or "we" feel, expect, hope, etc.) in the emission of well-defined messages, in the avoidance of false or oversimplified attributions (such as, "you *make* me mad"; "you *make* the children depressed"; "you *stop* me from sleeping at night," etc.), in the avoidance of global accusations (such as "you *never* showed me any real tenderness"; "you've *always* sabotaged my sense of identity"; "you've *always* avoided responsibility", etc.), in the avoidance of abstract language and the preference for precise and meaningful language, in listening to what the other says or is attempting to say, in affirming and validating his or her communication. Such communicational abilities, which every dialogue requires, can be learned in many contexts—individually, in groups, or in family therapy.

2. *Promoting willingness for dialogue.* Many adolescents and their parents lack such willingness: Their dissension is too great, and sufficient goodwill is lacking. In order to facilitate such a constructive and dialogic communication, it is necessary to understand the sources of dissent. This requires a new setting of our observational telescope, which is achieved by examining the relational modes of binding and expelling.

THE SECOND MAIN PERSPECTIVE: THE RELATIONAL MODES OF BINDING AND EXPELLING

Together with delegation, binding and expelling were presented in the original text as the three relational or transactional modes. I now use the term *transactional mode* only for binding and expelling. Delegation, which I formerly considered as an interactional mode located between binding and expelling, I now treat as an individual perspective. We are particularly concerned with it in this section.

Binding as a Result of Aborted Grief

In the original text I did not sufficiently emphasize an aspect of binding which contributes to almost every case of binding and indeed often plays a basic role—namely, unaccomplished work of mourning. Work of mourning was described by Freud in his classic study *Mourning and Melancholia* (1916). It involves parting and bearing pain, but also often the experience and working-through of many ambivalent and contradictory feelings, such as anger and disappointment, that we frequently associate with the mourned person or object. The separation process of adolescence also involves parents and children in the work of mourning. Both parents and children must give each other up in order to establish themselves on a new plane. Wherever an overstrong or pathological bond exists and continues, work of mourning will be neglected and indeed may have already been neglected, and therefore the work associated with separation is made more difficult or impossible.

It may be, for example, that one parent has not really parted from his or her own parents and remains bound to them. He then copes with and compensates for the unaccomplished work of mourning by a massive binding of another person, very often a child. The person with whom separation via grief work failed may already be dead. In such cases, the bound adolescent is often the substitute for the lost and ungrieved parent, sibling, or relative. From this point of view therapy consists primarily in the work of "unbinding" by making good the unaccomplished grief work. Two examples are Klaus and Sabine:

Klaus, a cherished only child who was one year away from his school-leaving exams, was unable to concentrate on his studies. Both he and his parents suffered great anxiety. Finally, he stopped attending school and, under pressure from his parents, consulted several psychiatrists, who indicated first a neurotic and then a psychotic disturbance. He then was admitted to the local psychiatric hospital. Here, for some months, he was given drug treatment with concomitant group therapy. Following his release from the hospital, he again attended school but seemed lethargic and remained aloof from his peers. In this situation both he and his parents decided on family therapy. For Klaus and his parents the turning point came when his mother, in a family session, was able to admit: "It's clear, my husband and I are really too bound up with Klaus. We don't leave him room to breathe. *Only it hurts so much to let him go.*" Coming to terms with this pain helped Klaus and his parents to unbind, to free themselves, and to find a new level of relatedness.

The case of sixteen-year-old Sabine shows how the neglected work of mourning, transferred to a substitute person and exaggerated, can prove binding. The "unbinding therapy" must attempt to make possible the neglected work of mourning in the original place with the original person.

Some nine months previous, two years from her school-leaving exam, Sabine had run away from home and become involved in the drug scene. A few days later she had come back to her parents, and from then on she slept most of the time at home, spending her days not at school, but loafing and drifting around with other dropouts. After her return home she began a round of consultations with a diverse selection of psychiatrists and psychologists.

It was clear even from the first family interview that Sabine provided her mother with a source of stimulation and worry that effectively "whipped" her out of a state of chronic depression. Since the death of Sabine's younger brother in a traffic accident, the mother had been locked into a rigid state of isolation, had alienated herself from her husband, and had only one remaining central relationship, with Sabine—who attempted to mitigate the isolation and give some point to her mother's existence. According to her own statements, the mother had at many times been on the brink of suicide. However, concern for her daughter drove away all thoughts of death and plunged her into a round of hectic activity: She made contact with teachers, psychologists, doctors, and acquaintances and, driven by their shared concern, began again to communicate with her husband without, however, achieving a solution. Nevertheless, Sabine had succeeded: Her parents had become closer, if only within the context she herself had created.

To unbind the mother and Sabine (and at the same time to release Sabine from the developmentally inappropriate and overburdensome delegation) it was also necessary to instigate a process of mourning which had previously been blocked. As the family together made good the neglected mourning, the binding between the mother and Sabine loosened and changed. Finally, Sabine went back to school and finished with satisfactory grades.

Further Considerations of Expelling

As we have seen, expelling, like binding, refers to an enduring and, as a rule, slowly developing relational structure which in contrast to binding, however, comprises a sustained neglect and devaluation of the expelled adolescent. Expelling is often found in broken families: Children of previous unions are a constant, irritating reminder (to the parent—who wishes to invest in new relationships, a new marriage, or new children) of the unpleasant past that she or he wishes to shake off. And it also occurs frequently in situations where women, as a result of overdemanding delegation, try, for example, to combine a strenuous career with a traditional housewife and mother role. If there is no alternative figure to whom the children can relate, such as a father or grandparents, they often suffer a greater or lesser degree of neglect.

Whatever the source of such neglect, the aim of the therapy is the same: the initiation or reestablishment of parental involvement with the children. In contrast to unbinding, this is work of constructing bonds. It is, in our experience, more difficult than work of unbinding, but it may also involve creating possibilities for making good unaccomplished mourning.

Often the expelled adolescent has lost his parents before he himself was able to take leave of them. In some crucial phase of his life, he had experienced his parents not being there for him without his being able consciously to realize and mourn this absence. He lacks living memories of conversations, common experiences, and confrontations which made or could make the parent real—that is, a finally accessible and emotionally invested relational partner. The therapeutic work of binding with expelled adolescents must first attempt as far as possible to make real the parents he lost or perhaps never actually had. It may involve the reestablishment of broken contacts, reunion, and final reconciliation; or may, as a precondition of leave-taking by the work of mourning, lead through reawakening of memories to "contact" with the lost parents or other important relational partners.

Work of binding often also means creating possibilities of lasting, trusting bonds through persons other than family members who in some way allow neglected relationships and experiences within the original family to be made good. This can be achieved by a careful and unobtrusive psychotherapy that offers the patient constant affirmation, such as is recommended by Heinz Kohut (1971) for certain narcissistic personalities (who, in my experience, are often expelled individuals). The following example illustrates therapeutic problems relating to expelled adolescents:

Hans, eighteen years old at the time of first contact, had left home two years before. He explained that life at home with his sister and unattached mother had become unbearable. His mother had more and more come to identify bad sides of his father in him: egotism, obstinacy, emotional coldness. When Hans was nine years old, the father, without any warning, had walked out into the night. Since then, there had been no contact with him: He might have emigrated, or he could have killed himself, or something else could have happened. Hans had only vague memories. In general, his picture of his father was negative, molded on what his mother so often told him.

In subsequent interviews, in the presence of the mother and sister, I discovered that the mother had met the father only a few months after the sudden death of her own father, and marriage had followed quickly. Her husband, being friendly and extroverted, had at that time seemed to resemble her dead father. But soon after the marriage, he had changed. He became sullen, egotistical, obstinate, and exploitative, so that family life became increasingly intolerable. She was therefore glad when one day he disappeared and for that reason had made no attempt to find him.

The mother showed most emotion when she spoke of the death of her own father. It quickly became clear that she had never really mourned his death and had never really taken leave of him. Almost without an interval, she had transferred to her husband the positive feelings she had for her father. Later, her suppressed disappointment and rage related to her father emerged directed against her husband—above all rage over her father's leaving her and exploiting her in a binding relationship. However, because she had never really experienced and worked through these feelings, she remained split: She debunked her husband while preserving the father's idealized image. Since no open communication between the married couple was possible, the mutual frustration and tension increased until the husband's final expulsion or flight. Soon after the father had left the home, the mother became involved with a new friend, who reminded her once again of her father's warm personality. The split negative feelings were now directed against her son, Hans, leading to *his* final expulsion.

The therapy had two principal aims: to enable the mother to make good the neglected work of mourning within her own family and to enable Hans to work toward a new bond with his father. Thus, Hans had to do everything possible to trace his father, however difficult this search would be. Nevertheless, by such a search, by such an investment in his missing father, Hans created the preconditions for true leave-taking from him. Without such a leave-taking, it could have been predicted that Hans would reenact his father's self-destructive pattern within his own relationships.

THE THIRD PERSPECTIVE: DELEGATION

Delegation, which in the original text formed an interactional mode between binding and expelling, now forms another main perspective. Within this perspective two therapeutically relevant aspects can be distinguished: *bound delegates* and *expelled delegates*.

BOUND DELEGATES

Bound delegates must perform missions that keep them within the family's emotional orbit. Such a mission might involve giving purpose to the life of one parent, in order to affirm the parent, care for the giver of the mission, and make sacrifices for him; or a bound delegate may have to embody the life of a deceased sibling and fulfill the expectations and ideals the family had for this sibling, thus sparing the parents the urgently necessary work of mourning. The case of Sabine described previously illustrates the predicament of such a burdened delegate.

EXPELLED DELEGATES

Expelled delegates suffer a different form of overdemanding delegation. As children they are comparatively less bound and at an early age experienced parental coldness and distance. Finally, they attempt to win a minimum of parental approbation and attention by the perfectionist fulfillment of certain parental expectations. I have found such delegation frequently in individuals suffering from cancer, who often seem delegated to develop self-effacing, conformist, and harmonizing personalities and may idealize their parents and others by whom they have been expelled and rejected.

Delegation and Triangulation

In the original text I described, among others, delegates who were given the mission by each parent to destroy the other. Such a conflicting and destructive delegation can, as I showed, place delegates in a desperate position from which the only release is psychosis or suicide.

Conflicting delegations arising from different mission givers occur whenever a third party is drawn into a one-to-one relationship, because it has become necessary to neutralize or stabilize this relationship. Here the family literature refers to *triangulation*. This always occurs when a child is used to supply sorrows and problems that divert the parents from their own mutual feelings of explosive rage and frustration. Instead of attempting to cope with their own problems and their mutual disappointment with one another, the parents quarrel over each other's methods of bringing up the child, or they use the child as evidence of the other's incompetence. A child caught in such a triangle is a bound delegate in the sense described above.

Therapeutic Consequences of the Delegational Model

The delegational model basically attempts to alter our perceptions of certain deviant forms of behavior (labeled as delinquent, psychotic, etc). Such behavior can be seen no longer simply as negative—for example, as expression of an ego or superego weakness, lack of self-control, suggestibility, psychological underdevelopment, psychopathology, etc.—but rather as a positive performance—indeed, possibly a sacrifice of the child for the parents and family. Sabine, previously described, who by flipping out staved off her mother's suicide, is an example. We can say that such delegates, by their deviant and often self-destructive behavior, frequently ensure the survival of one or both of the parents. At the same time, these delegates disburden the parents of anger, shame, and guilt. After all, the patient, the child, is the failure and not they, the parents. Further, he or she is often the only member of the family who is able to own and express the problems and conflicts which the others must disown and hide. He is therefore often the initiator and catalyst of a therapy from which all members of the family profit.

Within the framework of the delegational model, an escalating dynamic of mutual obstinacy and revenge frequently becomes visible. It is almost inevitable where the delegate bears ever greater demands yet is blamed for his wrong doing and is denied all recognition. It is precisely his service to the family and his mission of victim which then give him the possibility of loading the parents and other members of the family with shame, fear, and guilt. The fact that he is sick and disturbed reveals that his life is a failure and makes him the living proof of his parents' failure and badness. He operates a long "guilt lever," which allows him a dreadful and obstinate revenge for real or imagined parental exploitation.

The changed perceptions made possible by the delegational model also reveal the parents' need of help. The therapist can observe that not only the delegated child but also the parents are overburdened. He can recognize that they in their childhoods received from their own parents a heavy burden of disappointment, denied affection, injustice, rejection, undeserved trauma and loss—which they must in some way or another pass on to their own children. Either they attempt to recoup from their children what they missed in their own childhood or they try to exact from them the justice they themselves were denied.

The aim of therapy that emerges from the delegational perspective is the facilitation of dialogue that allows for confrontation as well as reconciliation. In the process, the parents learn to see their children with new eyes and, where possible, to recognize the sacrifices inherent in their various missions; the children, who also achieve a new view of their parents, learn to understand and, where possible, respect them. Once started, such a dialogue generally leads to a readjustment of expectations and a redistribution of missions within the family. Elvira, just fourteen years old, and her family illustrate important aspects of such a dynamic.

Elvira appeared along with her parents at the family interview. (Her only sister, who was seven years older, had stayed away to long after her sick fiancé.) The appointment for the interview had already been made several times with the mother and then put off. Each time, as the interview approached, Elvira had run off. Finally, all three appeared: husband, mother, and Elvira.

Elvira, wearing skintight jeans and platform shoes, sported violent scarlet lips and way-out curls. The mother—a well-educated secretary who had worked as a housewife for many years—showed the effects of many sleepless nights by the rings under her eyes. Elvira's father, a fifty-eight-year-old sawmill owner, stared sternly, but in a curiously detached way, around the room.

The mother first reported on the endless worries that Elvira had caused her parents in the last few years. She had fallen back at school, was under threat of being expelled, was considered a bad influence on the other children, and worse still, ran the risk of pregnancy and sexual disease by her nightly escapades with the most diverse and unsavory types of men. As the interview turned to Elvira's real or imagined sexual involvements, the expression of worry and exhaustion disappeared from her mother's face. She became, in contrast, vital and smiled continually at her daughter, with all trace of criticism gone. The father, with his stern and detached expression, seemed to be shut out from the female camaraderie.

Even in this first session the mother's unfulfilled sexual needs were discussed. I discovered that her husband was a war casualty and had high blood pressure. He was quite absorbed in his small business and, besides, watching television, had a regular meeting with a men's group. That was enough for him. His wife felt as if she had been put out to grass, doomed to a life without future, without meaningful or fulfilling activity, and lacking excitement and erotic tension. The latter was provided by Elvira, though in the tension that she provoked were mixed increasing elements of intransigence, provocation, and revenge, as might be expected within the framework of our delegational model.

In the course of several family sessions, which took place at intervals of from three to four weeks, the working focus moved from Elvira's sexual adventures to her parents' difficulties, and the girl's appearance changed almost out of recognition. She wore normal shoes, her comfortably wider jeans no longer carved her buttocks into folds, she used no make-up at all, and her previously untidy hair was washed. She gave the impression of being a "normal" though somewhat childish teenager interested in age-appropriate things which until now had been—neglected—cooking, looking after guinea pigs, and, last but not least, making good grades in school. But also the mother, since beginning to negotiate with her husband, seemed younger and less stiff and had bought herself a small secondhand car in order to look for a halftime job in the nearby town, where she hoped to build up a circle of friends.

THE FOURTH MAIN PERSPECTIVE: LEGACIES AND MERITS

The fourth main perspective also did not yet form a main concept when the original text was written. It was principally developed by Ivan Boszormenyi-Nagy (1973), who emphasized the importance of hidden loyalties and loyalty conflicts as a relational dynamic.

Delegation often involves a legacy handed down through generations; in this way delegational and multigenerational perspectives are related. Such a legacy may involve preserving the family—for example, by removing sources of family shame—supporting particular secular or religious values, or competing for success in particular areas such as politics, science, sports, or finance. Such legacies may become integrated into the personality in an ego-syntonic manner, or they can be ego-dystonic and then give rise to profound conflicts. This always occurs when there is what Ivan Boszormenyi-Nagy calls a legacy of split loyalties. The individual is delegated to embody the conflict of whole family clans as well as of their strife-ridden parents. Such, indeed, was the tragic destiny of Romeo and Juliet. Clinical experience has led me to understand many schizophrenic disturbances as not only the result and expression of massive binding and delegational dynamics but rather also of such legacies of split loyalty.

Within this multigenerational perspective and parallel to the concept of legacy is the central concept of merits. According to Ivan Boszormenyi-Nagy, the dynamic of important relationships includes a "ledger of merits." Therefore, merit or consciousness of merit is seen as a central motivational force in human relations comparable to that of drives or needs in psychodynamic (and especially psychoanalytic) theory. According to whether legacies are fulfilled or not, each member of the family has a positive or negative merit account. From this comes the consciousness of worth or integrity and the feeling of being justly or unjustly treated, of being able to make claims on the others or not, of having a meaningful or pointless existence.

The concept of the ledger of merits implies a force acting over generations and on all members of the family that compels each to settle his own accounts and insists that others settle theirs. When accounts remain unsettled there is a danger that communication may be broken off, trust lost, individual members of the family exploited, and the whole system corrupted; dialogue stagnates and negative replaces positive mutuality.

This perspective leads to the therapeutic aim of reestablishing or initiating dialogue—when necessary, including the grandparents—and in such dialogue discussing conflicitng legacies and unsettled ledgers of merits. One example is Erna—a young medical student, who lived in a conflict field of contradictory, multigenerationally conditioned legacies. Before her medical preexam (*Physikum*) she became tense and anxious, was unable to concentrate, and despaired at the idea of not being able to complete her course. Then suddenly one day she announced to her parents that she was pregnant and wanted to give up the course and get married.

In the family interview that followed these events, it became clear that the parents came from very different backgrounds. The mother's parents and grandparents were doctors, the father, on the other hand, came from a working-class family. The confusion after the war—both were refugees from the East—had brought the parents together. As the eldest child, Erna was delegated to achieve what her mother had been unable to do: to become a doctor. For the father, university and medical school represented a foreign world. He was warmer than his achievement-conscious, embittered wife, and Erna was grateful for his tenderness. Erna also felt emotionally attached to an uncle and aunt from her father's family. From early on, the father had made it clear to Erna that he feared a medical course would estrange her from his world. Erna's parents and grandparents had never discussed their different relationships with, and expectations of, the girl. In the interview it became clear how the conflicting, but never openly discussed, legacies had weighed on her. At the same time, the interview started a long overdue dialogue between the parents, which could aim to settle their respective ledgers of merits.

THE FIFTH MAIN PERSPECTIVE: STATE OF MUTUALITY

The fifth perspective only relatively recently became part of the Heidelberg model. The basis, however, was created earlier, above all by the late Gregory Bateson. Already in 1949 he described competitive contexts which "inevitably reduce the complex gamut of values to very simple and even linear and monotone terms" (Bateson 1972, p. 118). To simplify this, one may say that all such relationships are drawn into a power struggle. Bateson called such power struggle "symmetrical escalation." It resembles a form of an armament race where one protagonist, believing himself less equipped than the other, strives to get ahead, which causes the other to renew his efforts, and so on ad infinitum. Authors such as J. Haley (1963), P. Watzlawick (1967), and in particular M. Selvini Palazzoli (1978, 1980) investigated and followed up the mode and result of such armament races and power struggles in couple and family relationships.

With the help of the concept of negative mutuality, which I developed in 1971 (Stierlin, p. 60), important elements of this fifth perspective could be made more precise. Negative mutuality in terms of dynamic events or relational dynamic is the opposite of positive mutuality. Positive mutuality implies that the partners confirm and recognize each other on ever more complex and existentially meaningful levels. This means a true confrontation and final reconciliation become possible. In negative mutuality, the dialogic movement fails. Instead of mutual affirmation, the partners disqualify one another, and possibilities for true confrontation and reconciliation are restricted or lacking. I have termed the extreme form of power struggle developed from negative mutuality *malign stalemate*. The system here is totally hardened: Despite possible extremely dramatic external upheavals, the relationship does not change: The participants are in a clinch.

Elements of the other four perspectives already described are involved in this last main perspective. At the same time, it demonstrates a new relational mode and relational dynamic that primarily affects the "here and now," resulting in a malign clinch.

The image of boxers locked together can evoke this mode and relational dynamic. In such a clinch, the contestants often hit out wildly at each other but fail to shift the fight. It is impossible for them by their own strength either to loosen the clinch or to advance the contest. The fight levels off; the different differentiated strategies that reflect the individual expectations, aims, experiences, and life histories of the boxers are no longer expressed.

Unlike the prize fight, the clinch character of many relational situations is difficult to recognize. For example, a traditional individual-centered approach only brings one protagonist sharply into focus at a time, neglecting the other member of the system and their relationship. At the same time the weaponry provides a measure of variety in the relationship. It includes engendering feelings of helplessness and guilt in the opponent by playing out symptoms, weaknesses, and incompetence. It may mean disqualifying one's own communication and that of others; the construction of double-binds (relational traps); the avoidance of definition in the relationship, of leadership, and of personal responsibility; and the whole arsenal of often subtle tactics involving the use of power, devaluation, and demasking as shown in the increasingly voluminous literature about families. In particular, families with schizophrenic, anorectic, and chronically psychosomatically sick adolescents often demonstrate such a clinch or malign stalemate. The most important therapeutic aim in such families is to break the clinch so that there is a new chance for the relational forces directed toward growth, change, mutual definition of the relationship, and individuation.

The boxing analogy enables us to sketch some therapeutic consequences of this perspective. In boxing, it is the referee who usually loosens the clinch. Sometimes he has to intervene actively and energetically and quite literally apply his personal weight to the situation. Through such active personal action, he brings the match once again into motion and creates the scope for the unfolding of individuality and strategy, which fail as long as the clinch holds.

In my opinion, the family or couple therapist must intervene in a similarly active way, bringing the weight of his personality to bear. His authority lies in what I have called "the stronger person's reality" (1959). It can be most effectively applied when the therapist avoids all that might exacerbate the clinched patients' fears, insecurity, shame, and guilt. This is the value of what M. Selvini Palazzoli (1978) has called positive connotation, the giving of positive meaning—the ability or indeed art of the therapist that lies in the avoidance of even the slightest or most cryptic disapproval or stimulation of anxiety or guilt feelings and instead approves (almost) all the patients' actions. Both the active, intervening "stronger" reality of the therapist and the avoidance of fear or guilt arousal, create the optimal conditions for breaking up a malign clinch and power struggle.

TWO BASIC FAMILY THERAPEUTIC MODELS: HEALING THROUGH ENCOUNTER VERSUS HEALING THROUGH SYSTEMIC CHANGE

The five perspectives described provide a frame for therapeutic work with adolescents and their families. In any given case, this work can take very different courses. There exists as yet no standard settings or methods for doing family therapy comparable with those of psychoanalysis. Family therapists are at present unanimous only in agreeing on the basic principle that wherever an individual patient is treated the system of which he is part must be taken into account and, where possible, treated along with him.

In my opinion, family therapy is a basic concept within which there is scope for different forms of individual or group therapy according to the phases and aims of the therapeutic intervention. Wherever possible, we work from the beginning with all members of the system concerned, above all with the parents of the designated adolescent "patient" and his siblings.

The work of our Heidelberg family therapeutic group is currently directed by two important basic models or concepts: the models of *healing through encounter* (Begegnung) and *healing through systemic change.* We speak, therefore, of family therapeutic encounter or systemic work. The models have differences and similarities. Both require the therapist to show some form of "multidirectional partiality" (Ivan Boszormenyi-Nagy 1972): He must be able to develop a sympathetic understanding for the position of each member of the family, to put himself in that position, to be able to somehow like each member, and to be able to convey such liking. First and foremost, he must try to be just to the parents as well as to the adolescent. Both models also require that the therapist structures the family interaction during the session much more than during psychoanalysis; he must disrupt destructive patterns and act as an active director. The models demand, finally, that the therapist must, wherever possible, emphasize the positive and dismantle feelings of shame and guilt, especially for the parents. The differences between the models arise from the different aims that mold the conduct of even the first interview.

ENCOUNTER WORK

The encounter model endeavors to initiate a liberating, individuating, intrafamilial dialogue in the family session as rapidly as possible. The therapist makes it possible for the members of the family to discuss shame- and guilt-laden topics that have been, until now, taboo—such as family secrets, disappointed expectations, withheld justice, unshared, unaccomplished grief. He or she conveys, less by words than by actions and attitude, that we can discuss everything and survive all fears.

We can also say that to win the "battle for structure," as Carl Whitaker has described it (Napier and Whitaker 1978), the therapist, by example and will, makes possible the overdue intrafamilial discussion, reunion, and reconciliation. Usually, this concerns delegations and legacies that have been experienced as overdemanding and exploitative and unbalanced accounts of guilt, merits, abuses, and alienation. Three generations are often needed effectively to work through such abuses, missions, legacies, and accounts. This encounter work has important resemblances to psychoanalytical work: For both the arena and motor of the change are frequent therapeutic sessions. (Normally, psychoanalytical sessions are four times a week; family sessions, once a week only.) For systemic work the situation is different.

SYSTEMIC WORK

I am concerned here primarily with the systemic work of our Heidelberg team, which has much in common with the work of the Milan family therapeutic teams associated with M. Selvini Palazzoli and also, to a lesser extent, with the work of "systems therapists" such as S. Minuchin (1974) and J. Haley (1976, 1980), to whom we are indebted as well.

In our systemic work we aim to grasp as quickly as possible the important relational and systemic forces active in the family and to change them by maximal exploitation of the resources of a team of experienced therapists and observers, the observers holding a metaposition vis-à-vis the therapists and the family. They watch the family session from behind a one-way screen and note the reactions of the interviewers (therapists) and the family. The final intervention, worked out collaboratively, aims to effect systemic change and often takes the form of a paradoxical

*I cannot do justice to paradoxical prescriptions here; readers are referred to P. Watzlawick (1967, 1974), J. Haley, (1964, 1976), and M. Selvini Palazzoli et al (1977).

prescription.* These aims—the rapid grasp of the relational dynamic and the invention and implementation of a "clinch-breaking" intervention—are, in our experience, soonest met when the interviewer or therapist eschews all interpretation until the end of the interview. Wherever he or she senses resistance, he swims along with it, as it were. Above all, the therapist seeks information that illuminates the ways in which the members define their relationship to one another and how they form coalitions and/or triangulations. It is important to grasp whether these coalitions are overt or covert and whether they change or are fixed. Such information is often quickly available if each member of the family is asked what he or she thinks about the relational positions of the others. This is part of the circular interviewing technique, as developed and described by Selvini Palazzoli et al. (1980).

In contrast to the model of healing through encounter our model of healing through systemic change implies relatively long intervals of from four to six weeks between sessions. Having once laid the fuse designed to break the family out of their tight corner, the therapist must give the system time to change. In a stagnant family which has until now blocked every attempt of their growing children to separate, this may produce violent storms: A previously anorectic girl falls in love, experiments with sex, and stays away from home; the parents, left alone and unable to clutch at their child as problem provider, must confront their own problems and live out a midlife crisis.

Such massive, "clinch-breaking" interventions are, in my experience, indicated for strongly rigidified and bound families. This includes many families in which one member—usually an adolescent—has been diagnosed as schizophrenic or anorectic. We are concerned here particularly with rigidified and stagnant systems which constantly tend to stabilize in a state of negative mutuality.

Once the system is opened up, one must wait and see how far such a family frees itself, how far positive changes and individual individuation come into force without outside help. It may be that a new phase of therapy should begin, in which the adolescent who is primarily concerned catches up on social and practical experiences he has missed. Group or individual therapy may be most suitable. Sometimes the parents together need help to cope with the problems from which they have, until now, been diverted by the problems of their child.

Systemic Change and Facilitation of Dialogue

Finally, the systemic work, or perhaps one should say system-breaking work, I have described should make possible a liberating dialogue or positive mutuality. Often, the systemic work can be seen as preface to encounter work (to be carried out with or without therapeutic help).

Family therapy varies according to the phase of the process, the basic familial constellation (as revealed by the five main perspectives), and the therapeutic model (encounter or systemic) to be used. These differences notwithstanding, it is, for several reasons, nevertheless usually of shorter duration and more concentrated than individual-centered or, particularly, psychoanalytic therapy.

Above all, family therapy implies rethinking the type and the time span of the therapy required for the adolescent's problems. Comparison with psychoanalytic notions makes this clearer: Psychoanalysis reflects a Newtonian, rather than an Einsteinian, concept of energy. The Newtonian view implies opposing forces of equal strength. To change one force requires equivalent force or forces. This, for example, holds true for the psychoanalytic concept of "working-through." Deep-seated neurotic structures and behavioral patterns can accordingly only be altered by an expenditure of great amounts of time and energy, pitted against the patient's resistance in an extended working-through process—

which entails, among other things, the dynamics of transference and countertransference. The deeper and harder these structures are anchored in the personality, the more therapeutic work or "working-through" appears necessary.

Such a model of working-through may be contrasted with a cybernetic "field model." This is related not to mechanics, but to information theory. The basic concept here is that energy within individual systems is blocked or wrongly directed. What is needed is not massive inputs of energy from the outside, but rather new information which can remedy the blockage or misdirection of energy within the given systems. According to Gregory Bateson (1972), information is less a question of energy than of "a difference that makes a difference." This point of view implies that pathological and destructive relational patterns are often the expression of positive, but misdirected or perhaps "perverted," forces. Adopting this view, we may see, on closer observation, the apparently binding, intrusively exploitative, invalidating behavior of a member of a family as the expression of deep loyalty, of willingness for sacrifices, of love. It is the therapist's task to free such positive forces, to recognize them, or to help them to be recognized and thereby to mobilize the fallow or displaced resources in the family. This, too, differs from the psychoanalytic treatment model: A psychoanalyst, indeed any therapist working with individuals, must pay more attention to what happens between himself or herself and the patient, including the dynamics of transference and countertransference, than must a family or systems therapist, who needs to ask himself or herself continually where the unused resources of the family life—for example, in willingness for intervention or sacrifice, in readiness for confrontation or reconciliation—and how they can be identified and mobilized.

A short example (which, however, greatly simplifies the true complex relationships) can illustrate systemic work: Twenty-two-year-old Peter had been hospitalized several times in the last few years: His behavior was bizarre and extravagant; he had suddenly given up his work as a trainee and had spent money irresponsibly. His sister Margot, who was two years older, appeared, in contrast, competent and purposeful; she still lived at home. In the same household lived Peter's mother and his eighty-year-old grandmother, who had been cared for by her daughter for many years. It appeared that the grandmother, a chronic invalid, and her care were the center of his mother's life. The prospect that the old lady could die filled Peter's mother with perpetual, deep, unexpressed fear. She was only diverted from this fear when Peter gave her grounds for concern and provided herself and the family a focus of attention. On closer observation we found that Peter replicated many of the grandmother's symptoms in his own behavior and signs of disturbance. Like her, he spoke in a falsetto voice, acted in a silly fashion, and wasted the family money. Hence, our team based its paradoxical intervention on the following hypothesis: In this family, where over the generations one had to be either "caretaker" or "care receiver," Peter was preparing himself as the grandmother's death approached to take her place as "care receiver" and in this way sacrifice himself for his mother and the whole family. The team's prescription connoted positively such sacrifice and thus set the stage for Peter's rebelling against it, thereby changing the family's rule and fostering an individuating dialogue.

As the example of Peter shows, the crises of adolescence have a double aspect: They indicate that the necessary mutual process of individuation and reconciliation is in one or another way blocked or derailed, so that a negative instead of a positive mutuality develops and the dialogue between the generations is disturbed. Also, a crisis indicates the search for a solution. It can, indeed often must, imply that the members of the family have to adopt new rules, new points of view, and new methods of problem solving and communication—all of which can help to facilitate a dialogue which, in turn, propels the members' related individuation. As I see it, the family therapist's most important task is to be a facilitator of the overdue dialogue and to help in the search for new solutions.

FINAL REMARKS ON THE DIALOGUE BETWEEN THE GENERATIONS

In Western civilization at present, such a dialogue is more difficult than ever before. Accelerating social change—result and expression of worldwide technological change, economic interdependence, increasingly impersonal administrative structures, urbanization, population growth, expansion of mass media, with a deluge of information—has changed and continues to change radically the context of our lives and our relationships. It makes traditions, values, modes of thinking, and orientations, which the older generation believed it could or should transmit to the younger, problematic if not obsolete. It divides the experiential worlds of the generations and makes the task of finding a common focus of attention and language as a basis for dialogue ever more difficult. And yet, however difficult this dialogue may be for all participants—parents, adolescents, and therapists—it seems ever more necessary to give the drama of separation and reconciliation some chance for success.

References

Adelson, J.: The political imagination of the young adolescent. *Daedalus*, 100:1013–1050, 1971.

Ambrosino, L.: *Runaways*. Boston: Beacon Press, 1971.

Baldwin, J. M.: *Mental Development in the Child and the Race*. New York: Macmillan, 1895.

Baldwin, J. M.: *Social and Ethical Interpretation in Mental Development*. New York: Macmillan, 1899.

Baldwin, J. M.: *Genetic Theory of Reality*. New York: Putnam, 1915.

Bateson, G.: "Double Bind, 1969." Paper presented at the Symposium on the Double Bind, Annual Meeting of the American Psychological Association, Washington, D.C., September 2, 1969.

Bateson, G., Jackson, D., Haley, J., and Weakland, J.: Toward a theory of schizophrenia. *Behav. Sci.*, 1:251–264, 1956.

Bateson, G., Jackson, D., Haley, J., and Weakland, J.: A note on the double bind. *Fam. Proc.*, 2:154–161, 1963.

Bateson, G.: *Steps to an Ecology of Mind*. San Francisco: Chandler Publishing, 1972.

Becker, E.: *The Birth and Death of Meaning: A Perspective in Psychiatry and Anthropology*. New York: The Free Press of Glencoe, 1962.

Becker, E.: *The Revolution in Psychiatry*. New York: The Free Press of Glencoe, 1964.

Blos, P.: *On Adolescence: A Psychoanalytic Interpretation*. New York: The Free Press of Glencoe, 1962.

Blos, P.: *The Young Adolescent/Clinical Studies*. New York: Free Press, 1970.

Boszormenyi-Nagy, I.: "The Concept of Change in Conjoint Family Therapy." In A. S. Friedman, et al. (eds.): *Psychotherapy for the Whole Family*. New York: Springer, 1965(a), pp. 305–319.

Boszormenyi-Nagy, I.: "Intensive Family Therapy as Process." In I. Boszormenyi-Nagy and J. L. Framo (eds.): *Intensive Family Therapy*. New York: Harper & Row, 1965(b), pp. 87–142.

Boszormenyi-Nagy, I.: From family therapy to a psychology of relationships: Fictions of the individual and fictions of the family. *Compr. Psychiat.*, 7:408–423, 1966.

References

Boszormenyi-Nagy, I.: Loyalty implications of the transference model in psychotherapy. *Arch. gen. Psychiat.*, 27:374–380, 1972.

Boszormenyi-Nagy, I. and Framo, J. L. (eds.): *Intensive Family Therapy.* New York: Harper & Row, 1965.

Boszormenyi-Nagy, I. and Spark, G.: *Invisible Loyalties.* New York: Hoeber & Harper, 1973.

Bowen, M.: The family as a unit of study and treatment. *Am. J. Orthopsychiat.*, 31:40–60, 1961.

Bowen, M.: "Family Psychotherapy with Schizophrenia in the Hospital and in Private Practice." In I. Boszormenyi-Nagy and J. L. Framo (eds.): *Intensive Family Therapy.* New York: Harper & Row, 1965, pp. 213–243.

Bowen, M.: The use of family theory in clinical practice. *Compr. Psychiat.*, 7:345–374, 1966.

Brecht, B.: *Gesammelte Werke I.* Frankfurt: Suhrkamp, 1967.

Brodey, W. M.: Some family operations and schizophrenia. A study of five hospitalized families each with a schizophrenic member. *Arch. gen. Psychiat.*, 1:379–402, 1959.

Brown, C.: *Manchild in the Promised Land.* New York: Macmillan, 1965.

Bruch, H.: Conceptual confusion in eating disorders. *J. nerv. ment. Dis.*, 133:46–54, 1961.

Bruch, H.: Falsification of bodily needs and body concepts in schizophrenia. *Arch. gen. Psychiat.*, 6:18–24, 1962.

Bruch, H.: "Eating Disorders and Schizophrenic Development." In G. L. Usdin (ed.): *Psychoneurosis and Schizophrenia.* Philadelphia: Lippincott, 1966.

Butler, R. and Lewis, M. I.: *Aging and Mental Health: Positive Psychosocial Approaches.* St. Louis: C. V. Mosby, 1973.

Cole, L.: "Notes from Ralph." In L. Cole (ed.): *Street Kids.* New York: Ballantine Books, 1970.

Erikson, E.: *Childhood and Society.* New York: Norton, 1950.

Erikson, E.: *Identity and the Life Cycle.* New York: International Universities Press, 1959.

Fenichel, O.: *The Psychoanalytic Theory of Neurosis.* New York: Norton, 1945.

Fisher, S. and Mendell, D.: The communication of neurotic patterns over two and three generations. *Psychiatry*, 19:41–46, 1956.

Freud, A.: *The Ego and the Mechanisms of Defence.* New York: International Universities Press, 1946.

Freud, S.: *Mourning and Melancholia. Standard Edition*, 14: 237-258. London: Hogarth Press, 1957.

Freud, S. (1923): "The Ego and the Id." *Standard Edition*, 19:3–68. London: Hogarth Press, 1961.

Freud, S. (1933): "New Introductory Lectures." *Standard Edition*, 22:57–80. London: Hogarth Press, 1964.

Goffmann, E.: *The Presentation of Self in Everyday Life.* New York: Doubleday-Anchor, 1959.

References

Goffmann, E.: *Interaction Ritual.* New York: Doubleday-Anchor, 1967.
Goldfarb, W.: "Families of Schizophrenic Children." In L. C. Kolb, et al. (eds.): *Mental Retardation.* Baltimore: Williams & Wilkens, 1962. pp. 256–269.
Goldfarb, W.: The subclassification of psychotic children: Application to a study of longitudinal change. *J. Psychiat. Res.,* 6 (Suppl. 1): 333–343, 1968.
Goldfarb, W., Mintz, I., and Strock, K. W.: *A Time to Heal; Corrective Socialization: A Treatment Approach to Childhood Schizophrenia.* New York: International Universities Press, 1969.

Haley, J.: The family of the schizophrenic. A model system. *J. nerv. ment. Dis.,* 129:357–374, 1959.
Haley, J.: *Strategies of Psychotherapy.* New York: Grune and Stratton, 1963.
Haley, J.: *Problem-Solving Therapy.* San Francisco/Washington, London: Jossey Bass, 1976.
Haley, J.: *Leaving Home: The Therapy of Disturbed Young People.* New York: McGraw-Hill, 1980.
Hartmann, H.: Comments on the psychoanalytic theory of the ego. *Psychoanalytic Study Child,* 5:74–96, 1950.
Hegel, G. (1806): *The Phenomenology of the Spirit,* Translated by J. B. Baillie. London: Swann Sonnenschein, 2 volumes, 1910.
Hendin, H.: *Black Suicide.* New York: Basic Books, 1969.

Inhelder, P. and Piaget, J.: *The Growth of Logical Thinking from Childhood to Adolescence.* New York: Basic Books, 1958.

Jaques, E.: Death and the mid-life crisis. *Int. J. Psycho-Anal.,* 46:502–514, 1965.
Jenkins, R.: The runaway reaction. *Am. J. Psychiat.,* 128:168–173, 1971.
Johnson, A. and Szurek, S. A.: The genesis of antisocial acting out in children and adults. *Psychoanal. Quart.,* 21:323–343, 1952.

Kagan, J.: A conception of early adolescence. *Daedalus,* 100:997–1012, 1971.
Kilian, H.: *Das enteignete Bewusstsein.* Neuwied: Luchterhand, 1971.
Koestler, A.: *Darkness at Noon.* New York: Macmillan, 1941.
Kohlberg, L. and Gilligan, C.: The adolescent as a philosopher: The discovery of the self in a postconventional world. *Daedalus,* 100:1051–1086, 1971.
Kohut, H.: Forms and transformations of narcissism. *J. Am. Psychoanal. Assn.,* 14:243–272, 1966.
Kohut, H.: *The Analysis of the Self.* New York: International Universities Press, 1971.

Laing, R. D.: *The Self and Others: Further Studies in Sanity and Madness.* London: Tavistock Publications, 1961.
Laing, R. D.: Series and nexus in the family. *New Left Review,* 15:7–14, 1962.

Laing, R. D.: "Mystification, Confusion, and Conflict." In I. Boszormenyi-Nagy and J. L. Framo (eds.): *Intensive Family Therapy.* New York: Harper & Row, 1965.

Laing, R. D., Phillipson, H., and Lee, A. R.: *Interpersonal Perception.* London: Tavistock Publications, 1966.

Lessard, S.: America's time traps: The youth cult, the work prison, the emptiness of age. *The Washington Monthly,* 2:26–37, February 1971.

Levi, L. D., Stierlin, H., and Savard, R. J.: Fathers and sons: The interlocking crises of integrity and identity. *Psychiatry,* 35:48–56, 1972.

Lidz, T.: *The Family and Human Adaptation.* New York: International Universities Press, 1968.

Lidz, T.: *The Origin and Treatment of Schizophrenic Disorders.* New York: Basic Books, 1973.

Lidz, T., Fleck, S., and Cornelison, A. R.: *Schizophrenia and the Family.* New York: International Universities Press, 1965.

Lidz, T., Cornelison, A. R., Fleck, S., and Terry, D.: The intrafamilial environment of schizophrenic patients: II. Marital schism and marital skew. *Am. J. Psychiat.,* 114:241–248, 1957.

Lidz, T., Cornelison, A. R., Singer, M. T., Schafer, S., and Fleck, S.: "The Mothers of Schizophrenic Patients." In T. Lidz, S. Fleck, and A. R. Cornelison (eds.): *Schizophrenia and the Family.* New York: International Universities Press, 1965.

Mahler, M.: *On Human Symbiosis and the Vicissitudes of Individuation. Vol. I. Infantile Psychosis.* New York: International Universities Press, 1968.

Malcolm X.: *Autobiography of Malcolm X,* translated by A. Haley. New York: Grove Press, 1965.

Mendell, D. and Fisher, S.: An approach to neurotic behavior in terms of a three generation family model. *J. nerv. ment. Dis.,* 123:171–180, 1956.

Mendell, D. and Fisher, S.: A multi-generation approach to treatment of psychopathology. *J. nerv. ment. Dis.,* 126:523–529, 1958.

Meyers, D. and Goldfarb, W.: Psychiatric appraisal of parents and siblings of schizophrenic children. *Am. J. Psychiat.,* 113:902–915, 1962.

Minuchin, S., Montalvo, B., Guerney, B., Rosman, B., and Schumer, F.: *Families of the Slums.* New York: Basic Books, 1967.

Minuchin, S.: "Structural Family Therapy." In *American Handbook of Psychiatry,* Vol. II. New York: Basic Books, 1974, pp. 178–192.

Minuchin, S.: *Families and Family Therapy.* Cambridge: Harvard University Press, 1974.

Minuchin, S. et al.: *Psychosomatic Families: Anorexia Nervosa in Context.* Cambridge: Harvard University Press, 1978.

Napier, A.Y., and Whitaker. C.A.: *The Family Crucible.* New York: Harper & Row, 1978.

Nameche, G., Waring, M., and Ricks, D.: Early indicators of outcome in schizophrenia. *J. nerv. ment. Dis.,* 139:232–240, 1964.

Odier, C.: *Anxiety and Magic Thinking.* New York: International Universities Press, 1956.

References

Paul, N. and Grosser, G.: Operational mourning and its role in conjoint family therapy. *Community Mental Health Journal*, 1:339–345, 1965.

Pavenstedt, E.: A comparison of the child-rearing environment of upper-lower and very low-lower-class families. *Am. J. Orthopsychiat.*, 35:89–98, 1965.

Piaget, J.: *The Moral Judgment of the Child*. Glencoe, Illinois: Free Press, 1932.

Reich, C.: *The Greening of America: The Coming of a New Consciousness and the Rebirth of a Future*. New York: Random House, 1970.

Reiss, D.: Personal communication, 1970.

Reiss, D.: Varieties of consensual experience: Contrast between families of normals, delinquents, and schizophrenics. *J. nerv. ment. Dis.*, 152:73–95, 1971.

Ricks, D. F. and Berry, J. C.: "Family and Symptom Patterns that Precede Schizophrenia." In M. Roff and D. F. Ricks (eds.): *Life History Research in Psychopathology*. Minneapolis: The University of Minnesota Press, 1970.

Ricks, D. F. and Nameche, G.: Symbiosis, sacrifice, and schizophrenia. *Mental Hygiene*, 50:541–551, 1966.

Ricoeur, P.: *Freud and Philosophy*. New Haven, London: Yale University Press, 1970.

Sager, C., et al.: The marriage contract. *Fam. Proc.*, 10:311–326, 1971.

Schatzman, M.: Paranoia or persecution: The case of Schreber. *Fam. Proc.*, 10:177–207, 1971.

Scott, R. D. and Ashworth, P. L.: The 'axis value' and the transfer of psychosis. A scored analysis of the interaction in the families of schizophrenic patients. *Brit. J. med. Psychol.*, 38:97–116, 1965.

Scott, R. D. and Ashworth, P. L.: 'Closure' at the first schizophrenic breakdown: A family study. *Brit. J. med. Psychol.*, 40:109–145, 1967.

Scott, R. D. and Ashworth, P. L.: The shadow of the ancestor: A historical factor in the transmission of schizophrenia. *Brit. J. med. Psychol.*, 42:13–31, 1969.

Scott, R. D. and Montanez, A.: "The Nature of Tenable and Untenable Patient-Parent Relationships and Their Connection with Hospital Outcome." In D. Rubinstein and Y. O. Alanen (eds.): *Psychotherapy of Schizophrenia*. Amsterdam: Excerpta Medica, 1972, pp. 226–242.

Selvini Palazzoli, M., Boscolo, L., Cecchin, G., and Prata, G.: *Paradox and Counterparadox*. Jason Aronson, New York: 1978.

Selvini Palazzoli, M., Boscolo, L., Cecchin, G., and Prata, G.: Hypothesizing—circularity—neutrality: Guidelines for the conductor of the session. *Family Process*, 19:3–12, 1980.

Shainberg, D.: It really blew my mind. A study of adolescent cognition. *Adolescence*, 5:17–36, 1970.

Shapiro, R.: "Action and Family Interaction in Adolescence." In J. Marmor (ed.): *Modern Psychoanalysis*. New York: Basic Books, 1968.

Singer, M. T. and Wynne, L. C.: Thought disorder and family relations of schizophrenics. III: Methodology using projective techniques. *Arch. gen. Psychiat.*, 12:187–200, 1965(a).

Singer, M. T. and Wynne, L. C.: Thought disorder and family relations of schizophrenics. IV: Results and implications. *Arch. gen. Psychiat.*, 12:201–212, 1965(b).

Singer, M. T. and Wynne, L. C.: Principles for scoring communication defects and deviances in parents of schizophrenics: Rorschach and TAT scoring manuals. *Psychiatry*, 29:260–288, 1966.

Spitz, R.: Hospitalism: An inquiry into the genesis of psychiatric conditions in early childhood. *Psychoanalytic Study Child*, 1:53–74, 1945.

Stierlin, H.: The adaptation to the "stronger" person's reality. *Psychiatry*, 22:143–152, 1959.

Stierlin, H.: "Bleuler's Concept of Schizophrenia in the Light of our Present Experience." In *Third International Symposium on the Psychotherapy of Schizophrenia* (Lausanne, 1964). Basel/New York: Karger, 1965, pp. 42–53.

Stierlin, H.: Bleuler's concept of schizophrenia: A confusing heritage. *Am. J. Psychiat.*, 123:996–1001, 1967.

Stierlin, H.: *Conflict and Reconciliation.* New York: Doubleday-Anchor, 1969 (paperback); Science House, 1969 (hardcover).

Stierlin, H.: The functions of 'inner objects.' *Int. J. Psycho-Anal.*, 51:321–329, 1970.

Stierlin, H.: "Lyrical Creativity and Schizophrenic Psychosis as Reflected in Friedrich Hölderlin's Fate." In E. E. George (ed.): *Friedrich Hölderlin, An Early Modern.* Ann Arbor, Michigan: The University of Michigan Press, 1972(a), pp. 192–215.

Stierlin, H.: "The Impact of Relational Vicissitudes on the Life Course of One Schizophrenic Quadruplet." In A. R. Kaplan (ed.): *Genetic Factors in "Schizophrenia."* Springfield, Illinois: Charles C. Thomas, 1972(b), pp. 451–463.

Stierlin, H.: Interpersonal aspects of internalizations. *Int. J. PsychoAnal.*, 54:203–213, 1973.

Stierlin, H., Levi, L. D., and Savard, R. J.: Parental perceptions of separating children. *Fam. Proc.* 10:411–427, 1971.

Stierlin, H.: *Das Tun des Einen ist das Tun des Anderen.* Frankfurt: Suhrkamp, 1971. p. 60 ff.

Stierlin, H., Levi, L. D., and Savard, R. J.: "Centrifugal versus Centripetal Separation in Adolescence: Two Patterns and Some of Their Implications." In S. Feinstein and P. Giovacchini (eds.): *Annals of the American Society for Adolescent Psychiatry, Vol. II: Developmental and Clinical Studies.* New York: Basic Books, 1973, pp. 211–239.

Stierlin, H.: *Delegation und Familie.* Frankfurt: Suhrkamp, 1978.

Stierlin, H. et al.: *The First Interview with the Family.* New York: Brunner/Mazel, 1980.

Time magazine: "The Old in the Country of the Young." August 3, 1970, 49–54.

Watzlawick, P., Beavin, J.H., and Jackson, D.D.: *Pragmatics of Human Communication.* New York: W.W. Norton, 1967.

Watzlawick, P., Weakland, J.H., and Fish, R.: *Change.* New York: W.W. Norton, 1974.

Wein, B.: *The Runaway Generation.* New York: David McKay, 1970.

References

Welldon, R. M. C.: The "shadow-of-death" and its implications in four families, each with a hospitalized schizophrenic member. *Fam. Proc.*, 10: 281–302, 1971.

Winnicott, D. W.: "Aggression in Relation to Emotional Development." In *Collected Papers*. New York: Basic Books, 1958, pp. 204–218.

Wynne, L. C.: "Some Indications and Contraindications for Exploratory Family Therapy." In I. Boszormenyi-Nagy and J. L. Framo (eds.): *Intensive Family Therapy*. New York: Harper & Row, 1965, pp. 289–322.

Wynne, L. C.: Personal communication, 1971.

Wynne, L. C.: "The Injection and the Concealment of Meaning in the Family Relations and Psychotherapy of Schizophrenics." In D. Rubinstein and Y. O. Alanen (eds): *Psychotherapy of Schizophrenia*. Amsterdam: Excerpta Medica, 1972, pp. 180–193.

Wynne, L. C.: Schizophrenics and their families: I. Research re-directions. In press, *Brit. J. Psychiat.*, 1973.

Wynne, L. C. and Singer, M. T.: Thought disorder and family relations of schizophrenics: I. A research strategy. *Arch. gen. Psychiat.*, 9:191–198, 1963(a).

Wynne, L. C. and Singer, M. T.: Thought disorder and family relations of schizophrenics: II. A classification of forms of thinking. *Arch. gen. Psychiat.*, 9:199–206, 1963(b).

Wynne, L. C. and Singer, M. T.: Schizophrenics and their families: II. Recent research methods. In press, *Brit. J. Psychiat.*, 1973(a).

Wynne, L. C. and Singer, M. T.: Schizophrenics and their families: III. Recent Rorschach communication findings. In press, *Brit. J. Psychiat.*, 1973(b).

Wynne. L. C., Ryckoff, I. M., Day, J., and Hirsch, S. I.: Pseudo-mutuality in the family relations of schizophrenics. *Psychiatry*, 21:205–220, 1958.

Subject Index

Subject Index

Subject Index

Self-destruction, and "breakaway guilt," 50
Self-determination
  and cognitive binding, 41–42
  "obedient," 44–45
Self-image, and injected meaning, 43
Self-importance. *See also* Grandiosity
  narcissistic quest for, 154–155
  and runaway culture, 161
Self-observation
  and mission of delegate, 65
  substitute, 147
Self-sufficiency, premature, 106
Self-willed. *See* Egocentricity
Separation
  and binding mode, 37–38
  of centripetal couple, 33
  and cognitive binding, 41, 46–49
  conceptual model of, 4–9
  and conflict of generations, 180–183
  conflicts, displaced, 107
  of expelled adolescent, 119–120
  and exploitation of loyalty, 49–51
  ideal, 3
  and interplay of binding and delegating, 139–142, 184
  as "loving fight," 181–183
  via negative identity, 43
  parents' role in, 22–23
  premature, *xv*
  threat of, 102, 103–104
  transactional modes in, 123–127, 184
Sex. *See also* Promiscuity; Sexuality
  and adolescent crisis, 21
  and casual runaways, 17
  and centripetal couple, 32
Sexuality
  delegated, 61–62, 195–197
  and overgratifying parent, 39
  serving affective needs of parent, 56
Siblings of runaways, *xiii*
Silence
  and cognitive binding, 88–89
  of family member, 43–44
Slave. *See* Master-slave relations
Slights, overreactivity to, 154–155
Social change

  and liberation of parents, 176–179
  and runaway culture, 12–13, 29–31
Sociopathy
  of expelling parents, 164
  waywardness as, 156–159
Somatic complaints, 80
  and affective binding, 40–41
  of parents, 141–142
  and suicidal inclinations of mother, 82–83
"Spirit of Woodstock," 159
Street people, 69, 158
"Stronger reality," 36, 44–45, 97, 98, 202
Suicidal inclinations, 80, 93–94
  and breakaway guilt, 90, 138
  delegation to children of, 82–83
Superachieving student, 116–117
Superego, parental, and mission of delegate, 59–60, 64–65
Superego binding, 37, 38, 49–50
"*Superego lacunae,*" 59
Superstructure, 7
Survival
  and parents of wayward expellees, 162–165
  and runaway culture, 159–160
  and schizophrenia, 128
  and sociopathy, 158–159
Symbiotic phase of development, 130–131
Symbiotic union, 151
  "closure of," 136–138
  and schizophrenia, 130–131
Systems model, 6–7

Table manners, 40
Tension, and dialectical method, 8
Therapy. *See also* Family therapy
  and marital relationship, 171–173
  and mutual cognitive thralldom, 45
  and narcissism, 154–155
Three-generational approach, 169–170, 173–174, 181–182, 197–198
Thrills, vicarious, 55–56, 112, 149
Time magazine, 28 *n,* 162
Togetherness, and centripetal couple, 32

227

Name Index

D R. H ELM S TIERLIN earned both his doctorate in
philosophy and his medical degree in Heidelberg. He has held important positions in
German, Switzerland, and the USA, and has
lectured extensively in Australia, New Zea-
land, and the Scandinavian countries. Over the
years he has been affiliated with a number of
universities and research centers. Presently he is
the Director of the Psychosomatic Clinic,
University of Heidelberg.